BEHIND ENEMY LINES

HOW TO BE VICTORIOUS
IN THE ANTI-CHRIST
CULTURE OF THE ENDTIMES

Mike Kola Ewuosho

DESTINY IMAGE™ EUROPE srl
Via Maiella, 1
66020 San Giovanni Teatino (Ch) - Italy

"Changing the world, one book at a time."

This book and all other Destiny Image™ Europe books are available at Christian bookstores and distributors worldwide.

To order products, or for any other correspondence, please contact:

DESTINY IMAGE™ EUROPE srl
Via Acquacorrente, 6
65123 - Pescara - Italy
Tel: +39 085 4716623 - Fax: +39 085 9431270
E-mail: info@eurodestinyimage.com

Or reach us on the Internet: **www.eurodestinyimage.com**

ISBN: 978-88-89127-69-8

For Worldwide Distribution, Printed in Italy.
1 2 3 4 5 6 7 8/12 11 10 09

Dedication

I dedicate this work to our Lord Jesus Christ. His sacrifice and my receiving Him have brought an exciting life, full of faith adventures for me and many others through our ministries worldwide.

I dedicate this also to my wife and children. My wife has been an undeniable strength in what we are doing together. I have learned more about my temperament, and hence relationships, through her contributions. She has been a priceless asset in our life, ministries, and family.

I dedicate this as well to our spiritual family worldwide— especially our leaders who are doing great things for the Lord in their various regions of the earth. Your efforts, contributions, and labors inspire us to no little extent. Your sacrifices are definitely going to be rewarded by God.

Finally, I dedicate this to the entire Body of Christ world-wide, especially the leaders whose contributions have shaped the understandings and progress made in the Kingdom of God. Thank you for all your contributions.

Acknowledgments

Every book is the work of many people. Every author has been affected by many other authors; every leader has been inspired by other leaders. I am no exception. Many authors, as well as many preachers, have made indelible marks on my mind. And always, there are those who are closest and therefore make the greatest impact and possible contributions.

My wife, Olufunke, is closest to me and one of the great contributors into my life. In the midst of our busy schedule, we still make time for a face-to-face relationship. I am grateful to God for her many contributions to my life and the ministry we lead together. We make an unbeatable partnership in life and work of the ministry.

I would like to thank my editor and transcriber, Bisi Ilori, who is a pastor in our church—Word of Faith Christian Centre—in

Kano, Nigeria. I would also like to acknowledge our leadership teams in all the nations where we work, particularly in Nigeria and the UK, and especially our other pastors and their families: Wole Ogunnaike, Bayo Adenuga, Brown Ndubuisi, and Remi Owolabi—for the great contributions they are making to many lives in the Church in Kano. Your contributions are reaching the high heavens. I thank God for the contributions of our other pastors and their families in the nations of Ghana: Pastor Freduah Aggyemang-Appenteng; in Cameroon: Pastor Olivier Atemengue; and in Kenya: Pastor Job Simiyu. Pastor Raymond Uwuabor in Abuja, Pastor Sunday Ogundele in Suleja, and their families are also appreciated for their contributions.

I am also grateful to the leadership team over our church in Lagos, to members of all our churches, and to our partners around the world—your contributions have enabled us to come this far.

Finally, I want to acknowledge our lovely natural children: Sam, Keji, and Joan—for their love, support, and contribution to the work we are doing all over the world. Thanks to all.

Endorsements

The faithfulness and spiritual passion of Kola Ewuosho's ministry is a delight to behold. True servant-hearted, Bible-centered, and Christ-exalting leadership is needed in today's church. I'm pleased to recommend his words here. Kola is a friend who pursues the model of a leader described above, and does so with sincerity and devotion to Jesus' flock.

Jack W. Hayford
President, International Foursquare Churches
Chancellor, The King's College and Seminary

I had the honor of reading through the manuscript of *Behind Enemy Lines*. My heart leapt with joy at the privilege of holding in my hands truths that have been so graciously packaged for believers in these desperate and testy times that we are living in.

Many in the Body of Christ no longer submit to the unadulterated Word of God as the standard, which should govern their lives. They give the impression by their words and conduct, that the Bible is outdated and requires some updating, and that it is old-fashioned to serve God in sincere faith, with boldness in the Spirit, and godly character.

I have known the author since our teenage years, and I have observed the sincerity of his faithfulness to Christ. He is a man who doesn't just practice what he preaches, but indeed preaches what he practices. I thank God for the day He commissioned Rev. Kola Ewuosho to bring such a timely message as *Behind Enemy Lines* to this generation. You now hold in your hands a God-ordained script that is capable of motivating and challenging you from an ordinary life, into an extraordinary one reminiscent of believers living in New Testament times. The principles are so clearly presented and are easy to follow. Get ready to not only be blessed, but to be a blessing.

It is without hesitation that I highly recommend *Behind Enemy Lines*.

Pastor Inyang Okutinyang
Senior Pastor, Faith Foundation Fellowship
Sarnia, Canada

Table of Contents

Foreword

I have had the joy and privilege to know the author, Kola Ewuosho, for almost 20 years. Without a doubt, I can say that there are only a few people who I know as closely as I know him, and I honor the grace of God upon his life. I have been around him under different conditions starting from his platform, Word of Faith Christian Center in Kano, Nigeria. In addition, I have traveled with him on some difficult mission assignments where we lived under extremely hard and strenuous conditions as we did in Cote d'Ivoire. I have also been with him in his new assignment as set minister of Harvestime Church in Virginia Water, Surrey, UK.

The content of this book is very characteristic of the author. I say so because in the myriad of discussions we have had on extremely difficult topics, it has always been evident that the wisdom of God exudes out of his mouth.

Behind Enemy Lines, in my opinion, is a wake-up call. I am reminded of Numbers chapter 10, with emphasis on verses 2 and 8. "Make two silver trumpets for yourself; you shall make them of hammered work; you shall use them for calling the congregation and for directing the movement of the camps. ... The sons of Aaron, the priests, shall blow the trumpets; and these shall be to you as an ordinance forever throughout your generations" (NKJV).

God used the trumpet to lead Israel (the church in the Old Testament), who though had been delivered from the bondage of Egypt for many years, still found themselves entangled in the wilderness journey. Although there were many uses for the trumpet, two distinct uses stand out. The trumpet was used for calling the congregation and for directing the movement of the camp. Indeed, it was the intervention of God through the making of the trumpet that was ultimately instrumental in bringing them to their promised land, the place of victory.

There is no better time than now for the remnant Church to stand up. It is in these days of global economic meltdown that the Daniels and the Josephs indeed shine forth. It is in this season that God raises up His best. It is time for the Church to operate from *Behind Enemy Lines* and take back territories from the enemy.

This book is a must-read for every leader and every believer. I pray that as you read it, you will willingly accept the challenge it poses and receive the grace to work in it. By so doing, we will leave our mark and become catalysts for change in this generation.

Bank Akinmola, President
World Outreach Missions, Inc., USA

Preface

I hear the sound of a distant drum. The sound of divine discontentment is rising in many hearts as people see the enemy carry out his onslaught on the Body of Christ and the world at large.

There is a cry in the spirit: "Where are the Daniels? Where are the Esthers and Josephs of this generation? Who will arise and say, 'If I perish, I perish'? Who will purpose in their hearts not to defile themselves? Who will go for us, and whom will we send? Who will bear the tidings of living out the lifestyle of the Kingdom of God in the midst of Babylon or the kingdom of darkness?"

Where is the power we read about in the Bible? Where is the power of godly purpose seen in Joseph, who refused to be bitter against his brothers? Where is the power of consecration we read about in Daniel, who purposed in his heart not to defile himself in Babylon? Where is the power of focus we see in apostle Paul, who refused to give up in the face of opposition and hardship?

These questions are beginning to arise in our minds as we contemplate events that are taking place around the world today. How can the power of God be so undermined in countries that were once sending the Gospel to other nations?

God is in the business of recovery. The need for repentance and returning to the ways of the Lord cannot be overemphasized. The need to be reconciled back to God as we turn from our wicked ways becomes vital to our survival as Christians. The need to reexamine our ways and hearts before God, in sober reflection and seeking to make amends, is crucial in these days. God is still searching for those whose hearts are upright so He can show Himself strong on their behalf. This book is asking that we hear the clarion call—to separate ourselves from ungodly ways of thinking and acting—and rise with strength from within, to be and do all God has for us.

The secret of strength in God is found in our everyday activities. It's not what we do occasionally that produces lasting results but what we do regularly. What has defined our everyday living? What stronghold has held our minds in bondage? What has affected our expectations, orientation, and perspectives? These need adjustment from time to time. It's time we stop allowing the enemy to determine these things in our lives.

We need to cultivate standards of living based on biblical principles, and allow insight from God's Word to inform our decisions, as we make the choices that will position us to experience God's power regularly in our lives. This is what this book is about.

This book is based on a series of messages entitled, "End-time Secrets From the Life of Daniel." I pray the Lord will grant you insight into His plans and purposes for your life. I also pray that there will be an impartation in your life, so you will be a doer and not just a hearer. I believe and thank God, in advance, for this and much more in your life.

Post Scriptum: This book was submitted in its original draft to the publisher months before the outbreak of the credit crunch and recession hitting the world's economies. This predicament is a good example of a situation that defies human solution and presents another opportunity for the Daniels to arise with godly wisdom, showing God strong on our behalf, and bringing about lasting power.

Mike Kola Ewuosho

Prologue

GRACE FOR THE JOURNEY

"Grace is…the essence of the power to live a life of holiness before God."[1]

As we begin this journey together, we need to understand the place of God's grace. We all have often had God's Word spoken to us, read a difficult and challenging truth in the Bible or in books written by men and women inspired of God. At times, instead of what we have heard or read inspiring hope and courage in us, it produces despair and discouragement. We read and we hear and we wonder, *Will I ever be able to live by the demands of the truth I have just heard? Can I do what I have read?* We know we have encountered truth, but the demands the truth is making on us seem so great that we despair and lose courage. Could this be what happened to the disciples of Jesus who left Him? It says in John chapter 6 that Jesus had just spoken these words to them:

> *Then Jesus said unto them, Verily, verily, I say unto you, Except ye eat the flesh of the Son of man, and drink His blood, ye have no life in you. Whoso eateth My flesh, and drinketh My blood, hath eternal life; and I will raise him up at the last day. For My flesh is meat indeed, and My blood is drink indeed. He that eateth My flesh, and drinketh My blood, dwelleth in Me, and I in him* (John 6:53–56).

We need to keep it in mind that Jesus Himself is truth, and what He says is truth (see John 14:6; 8:45). These words were truth from the lips of the Savior Himself. But what was the reaction of a majority of the disciples to the truth they heard from the truth Himself?

> *Many therefore of His disciples, when they had heard this, said, This is an hard saying; who can hear it?…And He said, Therefore said I unto you, that no man can come unto Me, except it were given unto him of My Father. From that time many of His disciples went back, and walked no more with Him* (John 6:60;65–66).

From these passages of Scripture, it is clear that truth does not always produce a positive effect. On another occasion, after Jesus had told people the truth, they became so angry that they wanted to kill Him! (See Luke 4:28-29.)

However, even though many of His disciples left Him in the John 6 account, there were some who received the same truth and stayed. What was working in them that caused the truth to have a different effect?

> *Then said Jesus unto the twelve, Will ye also go away? Then Simon Peter answered Him, Lord, to whom shall we go?*

Thou hast the words of eternal life. And we believe and are sure that Thou art that Christ, the Son of the living God (John 6:67-69).

Truth is meant to set us free, not to discourage or condemn. However, there must be work done in us to position us to receive truth when it comes. Jesus said, "No man can come to Me except it were given unto him of the Father" (John 6:65). What does the Father give that makes it possible for us to receive truth?

Peter had a revelation of who Jesus was. He knew He was the Christ! The revelation Peter had made him understand he was not listening to the words of a mere human being. He received the word Jesus spoke as the Word of God. This revelation produced grace in the life of Peter. It takes grace to be able to receive and walk in the demands of truth. Without grace we will not be able to do the things truth demands of us.

One of the ways grace comes to us is through the revelation of Jesus Christ. As it says in First Peter, "Wherefore gird up the loins of your mind, be sober, and hope to the end for the grace that is to be brought unto you at the revelation of Jesus Christ" (1 Pet. 1:13).

We should also keep in mind that Jesus said we cannot come to Him except it is given of the Father. It was the Father who gave Peter the revelation of Jesus, and this is why he could receive the truth—it was given by the Father!

He saith unto them, But whom say ye that I am? And Simon Peter answered and said, Thou art the Christ, the Son of the living God. And Jesus answered and said unto him, Blessed art thou, Simon Barjona: for flesh and blood hath not revealed *it unto thee, **but My Father** which is in heaven* (Matthew 16:15-17).

There was grace at work in the life of Peter, which was produced by the revelation of Jesus Christ. Obviously, the others did not see Jesus the same way. This was why it was difficult for them to receive truth. "And they said, Is not this Jesus, the son of Joseph, whose father and mother we know? How is it then that He saith, I came down from heaven?" (John 6:42). They knew Jesus after the flesh, not by revelation; grace was not at work in them at that time. We need to understand this clearly. The key to receiving truth and living it is in the working of grace in our lives. Grace is a critical component of being His disciples.

God's Word will always impose a responsibility on us. Many times God will use a man or woman to bring His Word to us. Our first responsibility is to receive the Word as His Word and not the Word of a mere human being. It is only when we receive the Word as the Word of God, and not of man, that we will be in a position to respond to that Word.

> *For this cause also thank we God without ceasing, because, when ye received the word of God which ye heard of us, ye received it not as the word of men, but as it is in truth, the word of God, which effectually worketh also in you that believe* (1 Thessalonians 2:13).

The church in Thessalonica received the Word that apostle Paul spoke as the Word of God not man. This is why the Word was effectual in its working in them. Often, we consider messages or books to be the authors' own ideas or good reasoning. I do not believe it should be so! The Word must be received and believed as the Word of God for it to work effectively in us. Receiving the Word as God's Word immediately unlocks the potential in the Word that only God can release. Our faith must be in the power of God, not in the wisdom of men (see 1 Cor. 2:5).

After receiving God's Word, it is important that we spend time meditating on what we have believed and received. It is the process of prayerful meditation that causes God's Word to take its root deep into the soil of our heart. Persecution will come for the Word's sake. Going through persecution at such times is part of the process God expects us to submit to. Unless we realize this, we will easily be offended when such persecution comes (see Mark 4:17).

The condition of our hearts can influence how fruitful the Word of God will be in our lives. God expects us to deal with the condition of our hearts—to address all internal issues that have the ability to affect the productivity of God's Word in us. Regarding the heart, the Bible clearly states that "out of it are the issues of life" (Prov. 4:23). The condition of our hearts will, to a large extent, determine whether or not we will be able to bear the fruit of the Word we have received.

There are many issues that if not dealt with can affect our productivity. Cares, distractions, bitterness, and unforgiveness are just a few. Such issues, unknown to many of us, create a climate that is not conducive to nurturing of God's Word. If these internal issues are not dealt with, we will be frustrated and keep wondering why it seems the Word of God is not doing much in our lives.

After receiving the Word as from God, not man, engaging in prayerful meditation, and dealing with the condition of our hearts, we need to take the last step and bear fruit. God's Word is a seed that comes into our hearts, and that seed is meant to produce fruit. We are the ones with the responsibility of bearing fruit. In essence, we must apply our faith and love to ensure that what we have received is producing results in us. Bearing fruit is not a passive activity. We must be actively involved. Our faith and love must be engaged; we must put the Word in our mouth as our confession and carry an attitude that creates a climate for God's Word to produce. Many times we wait on God expecting God to do the work, but God is waiting on us.

The process of bearing fruit is beautifully described in Mark chapter 4:

Hearken; Behold, there went out a sower to sow: And it came to pass, as he sowed, some fell by the way side, and the fowls of the air came and devoured it up. And some fell on stony ground, where it had not much earth; and immediately it sprang up, because it had no depth of earth: But when the sun was up, it was scorched; and because it had no root, it withered away. And some fell among thorns, and the thorns grew up, and choked it, and it yielded no fruit. And other fell on good ground, and did yield fruit that sprang up and increased; and brought forth, some thirty, and some sixty, and some an hundred. And He said unto them, He that hath ears to hear, let him hear. And when He was alone, they that were about Him with the twelve asked of Him the parable. And He said unto them, Unto you it is given to know the mystery of the kingdom of God: but unto them that are without, all these things are done in parables: That seeing they may see, and not perceive; and hearing they may hear, and not understand; lest at any time they should be converted, and their sins should be forgiven them. And He said unto them, Know ye not this parable? And how then will ye know all parables? The sower soweth the word. And these are they by the way side, where the word is sown; but when they have heard, Satan cometh immediately, and taketh away the word that was sown in their hearts. And these are they likewise which are sown on stony ground; who, when they have heard the word, immediately receive it with gladness; And have no root in themselves, and so endure but for a time: afterward, when affliction or persecution ariseth for the word's sake, immediately they are offended. And these are they which are sown among thorns; such as hear the word, And the cares of this world, and the deceitfulness of riches, and the lusts of other things entering in, choke the word, and it becometh unfruitful. And these are they which are sown on good ground; such as hear the word, and receive it, and bring forth fruit, some thirtyfold, some sixty, and some an hundred (Mark 4:3-20).

In this parable, Jesus shows us the process that the Word of God must go through to be fruitful in us. Verse 20 is very instructive as it shows that we are to bring forth fruit. I have said it earlier, and I will say it again. We have the responsibility of bearing fruit, not God. Once the Word is sown, the fruitfulness of the Word is no longer determined by the sower; it is determined by the soil.

Every Word we receive is supposed to produce fruit in our life. There is fruit for every Word we receive. This is why when we read a book or hear the Word of God, we know deep down in us that a demand has been placed on us to do something with what we have heard. We are expected to be fruitful! It is when we measure this demand against our natural human ability that discouragement sets in. Usually, we see ourselves as being so far from the standards God expects from us that we lose hope. This does not have to be so.

The text you will be reading in this book will be very challenging. These truths will challenge what you have believed, how you think, and your actions. After reading this book, you may wonder if you will ever be able to live up to the standards and lifestyle of a Daniel in Babylon—a Christian living in an alien anti-Christ culture.

We have good news for you! It is not going to be by your own power or might; it is going to be by God's grace. God's grace has been given to us to empower us to live our daily lives according to what the truth demands of us. In his book, *A Heart Ablaze*, John Bevere states it this way: "…for grace is His bestowed ability to do what His truth demands. It empowers us to obey God's words."[2]

This indeed is one of the main differences between the old and new covenants. Under the old covenant, the law was given and it proved everyone guilty (see Rom. 3:19). No one was able to live according to the standards of the law. The law itself was good, as apostle Paul acknowledges in Romans 7:12, but the people to whom it was given lacked the ability to live according to the demands of the law. The law simply left everyone guilty.

Many times we still receive the Word of God with the mind-set of a person under the law. We receive God's Word as an external imposition rather than an internal working of the Spirit. But the Bible says, "For it is God which worketh *in you* both to will and to do of His good pleasure" (Phil. 2:13).

In the new covenant, God works first of all *in us*, before working *through us*. When the truth comes to us, God's desire and design is to give us the grace we need to do what the Word (His truth) demands. This is one of the reasons why God's Word is called "the word of His grace" (see Acts 20:32).

John chapter 1 says, "For the law was given by Moses, but grace and truth came by Jesus Christ" (John 1:17). God, through His Son Jesus Christ, has released a dispensation of grace upon humanity. Jesus is described as being "full of grace and truth," and we are told that "of His fulness have all we received, and grace for grace" (see John 1:14,16).

There is an intimate relationship between grace and truth. As mentioned earlier, grace is a distinguishing feature between the old and new covenants. In the new covenant what truth demands, God gives grace to obey. What then is the grace of God? John Bevere writes:

> A deceptive thought process is present in our modern church. It has been conceived and brought forth by an unbalanced teaching of grace. Most often grace is referred to as an excuse or cover-up for a life of worldliness. To put it quite bluntly it is used as a justification for self-seeking, fleshly lifestyles. Too many Christian groups have over emphasized the goodness of God to the neglect of the Holiness and Justice. This swing to the extreme left has caused many to have a warped understanding of the grace of God.[3]

Truly, many people have used grace as a big cover-up for a lifestyle of looseness and lasciviousness, claiming they are pardoned or covered by grace. But is this what *grace* means?

The word *grace* as used in this context is from the Greek word *charis*. *Strong's Bible Concordance* describes *grace* as "the divine influence upon the heart and its reflection in the life."[4] This definition reveals that grace is an influence that produces a visible result in the life of the one who has grace. In other words, grace is visible.

25

As it says in the Book of Acts, "Who, when he came, and had seen the grace of God, was glad, and exhorted them all, that with purpose of heart they would cleave unto the Lord" (Acts 11:23). According to this verse, Barnabas saw the grace of God. How was this grace manifested? Among other things, it was manifested in their obedient lifestyle. They were obedient to the truth they had received.

Before going any further, I do need to point out that there are many facets or dimensions of the grace of God. God Himself is multi-dimensional, and the things of God have that same characteristic. For instance, salvation is multi-dimensional. We have been saved, we are being saved, and we shall be saved. There is a past, present, and future dimension to salvation. Holding on to only one or two dimensions of salvation will not be holding on to the complete truth. Even though it is true that we have been saved from our sins through the redemptive work of Christ on the cross at Calvary, our souls are still in the process of being saved, and our bodies shall be redeemed (see 1 Pet. 1:9; Rom. 8:23; James 1:21).

If we act as if there is only one dimension to God or the truth of His Word, we are being narrow-minded and very shortsighted. We can get the complete picture only by putting all the dimensions together. I am saying this because I want to make clear that I do know there are other dimensions to the grace of God. But I am writing here about the dimension of grace that enables us to do what God's truth demands of us.

God wants us to be able to live by His Word. He does not want the demands of His Word to be an external imposition but an internal delight. He wants sons and daughters who rejoice at His Word.

Grace is God's influence on the heart of a man or woman, and it is reflected in that person's life. When we are living by His grace, we have the strength to live by the Word of God and say, "No!" to sin. The Bible says, "For the grace of God that bringeth salvation hath appeared to all men, teaching us…" (Titus 2:11-12).

God is bringing truth to us, but the truth is accompanied by grace. There is no need for despair or discouragement when we know that the same One who places a demand on us by His Word, supplies the grace to do what His Word demands. God is for us, not against us. His love and mercy have made a provision for us to live in victory. As He did not withhold His only begotten Son, we should be confident that God will not withhold anything we need to live a victorious Christian life.

As we take this journey together, let us be strong in the grace of God, let us be confident in the assurance of the Father's love for us, and let us step out in faith as bold doers (not just readers) of the Word of God.

ENDNOTES

1. John Bevere, *A Heart Ablaze* (Nashville, TN: Thomas Nelson, Inc., 1999), 95.
2. Ibid, 97.
3. Ibid, 98.
4. *Strong's Exhaustive Concordance of the Bible* (Peabody, MA: Hendrickson Publishers), 77.

Introduction

Behind enemy lines! Enemy territory is not a place most people go willingly. Even soldiers seasoned in warfare know the rules of warfare change when in enemy territory. When behind enemy lines, the enemy is in charge, the enemy makes the rules, and the enemy is out to resist and destroy any opposition. As Christians, we must wake up to reality: We are living behind enemy lines! Just like Special Forces who are equipped to infiltrate and win behind enemy lines, God has equipped His Church to overcome in enemy territory.

There is a general manual that contains guidelines to prepare and train soldiers for war; however, Special Forces have a special manual and special training. The Book of Daniel is more than just an interesting book; it is a manual for training. It is a book that contains mysteries meant to be revealed for the benefit of the Church today and for the advancement of God's Kingdom. If studied and meditated upon, the Book of Daniel will cause believers to be winners behind enemy lines.

Daniel represents the Church of God in these last days. Daniel was a Jew—a covenant child of God—who had been captured, made a slave, and brought right into the middle of an idolatrous and pagan nation. In a sense, he was behind enemy lines. Despite his position and location, Daniel operated by principles that made him an overcomer in a system that was contrary to everything he believed and stood for. In slavery to a foreign king, he learned to walk in victory over the system. He overcame the influence of Babylon, and eventually subjected the entire Babylonian system to the God he served. This is the position and place the Church must take in the times in which we live.

God has reserved the same spirit, grace, anointing, and character that Daniel had for the Church today. It will take a similar enabling power (grace) that Daniel received and operated in, for the Church to stand strong and overcome the forces of hell, which have been unleashed against the Body of Christ.

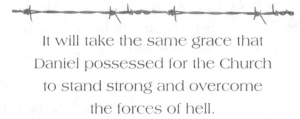

It will take the same grace that
Daniel possessed for the Church
to stand strong and overcome
the forces of hell.

The Church today is in a society that is anti-God. God and the things of God are ridiculed and looked down upon daily. Scandals among leaders in the Body of Christ and in churches around the globe have not made things better. We are in a culture that not only despises the things we ought to hold dear but actively resists that for which we stand. Isaiah still shouts with a loud voice today:

No one calls for justice; no one pleads his case with integrity. They rely on empty arguments and speak lies; they conceive trouble and give birth to evil. They hatch the eggs of vipers and spin a spider's web. Whoever eats their eggs will die, and when one is broken, an adder is hatched. Their cobwebs are useless for clothing; they cannot cover themselves with what they make. Their deeds are evil deeds, and acts of violence are in their hands. Their feet rush into sin; they are swift to shed innocent blood. Their thoughts are evil thoughts; ruin and destruction mark their ways. The way of peace they do not know; there is no justice in their paths. They have turned them into crooked roads; no one who walks in them will know peace. So justice is far from us, and righteousness does not reach us. We look for light, but all is darkness; for brightness, but we walk in deep shadows. Like the blind we grope along the wall, feeling our way like men without eyes. At midday we stumble as if it were twilight; among the strong, we are like the dead. We all growl like bears; we moan mournfully like doves. We look for justice, but find none; for deliverance, but it is far away. For our offenses are many in your sight, and our sins testify against us. Our offenses are ever with us, and we acknowledge our iniquities: rebellion and treachery against the Lord, turning our backs on our God, fomenting oppression and revolt, uttering lies our hearts have conceived. So justice is driven back, and righteousness stands at a distance; truth has stumbled in the streets, honesty cannot enter. Truth is nowhere to be found, and whoever shuns evil becomes a prey… (Isaiah 59:4-15 NIV).

God knew that such a time and age would come. That is why He ordained that among the cloud of witnesses cheering us on, the voice of Daniel and his three friends can be clearly heard today. What are their voices saying? What are the principles they embraced that gave them victory and made them overcome in a society and culture that had no respect or value for the God they loved and served?

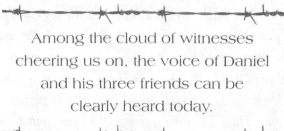

Among the cloud of witnesses
cheering us on, the voice of Daniel
and his three friends can be
clearly heard today.

The different types of anointing and grace that God releases on His servants do not leave the earth when those servants depart. The anointing and grace stay here on earth. Any anointing or grace that was evident in the life of any of God's servants is still available for us today. The same anointing that was upon Daniel and his friends is still available to us. The question is: How do we access this grace?

Maybe you are like most Christians. Perhaps you have asked the question, too: Is it possible for a Christian to live right and victoriously in the world we live in today? I believe with all my heart that the answer is YES! And I believe we can find the answer in a study and application of the principles that governed the life of Daniel and his three friends.

I believe the Book of Daniel holds some keys to enable the emerging of a victorious Church and citizens of the Kingdom of God today. In this book, God has given us keys to win behind enemy lines!

There are so many features to examine in the life of Daniel, so many principles to learn and practice. Daniel obviously had knowledge of God that is beyond mere knowledge about God. He knew God, and he knew how to function within the context of his knowledge of God's will for his time. He had incredible access to things in the spirit that were strange to others. The things he was able to access in the spirit made a world of difference as to how he operated and the victories that he enjoyed. He also had good knowledge of how to operate successfully on the earth without breaking God's laws, both written and inferred. He functioned so excellently in all areas of his life that there was no fault found in him by anyone. He was prophetic, academically sound, and socially aboveboard. And he understood principles without yielding to religious spirits seeking to undermine true spirituality.

What were the secrets? What were the principles Daniel knew and lived by? That's what this book is about. Let us go on an adventure together—a journey into the past to discover truth for today. Remember, the truth we know and live by will make us free. The truth that sets us free is the truth that confronts the true state of our hearts. Today, it is time to enter into the glorious liberty of the sons of God. Let us study the life of Daniel from the first 6 chapters of the Book of Daniel, and see how to live victoriously and win behind enemy lines in these endtimes.

Consecration

God is calling aside His people, separating them from the world, and creating a covenant mind-set in them for exploits for the Kingdom.

What if we were to try to put a finger on one thing in the life of Daniel that made the difference between success and failure, between overcoming and being overcome, and between fulfilling destiny and failing to fulfill destiny? If we could try to discern his greatest asset, what do you think it would be?

I believe Daniel's greatest asset was his consecration to God. In Daniel chapter 1, we can see a glimpse of the level of this consecration to God. "But Daniel resolved not to defile himself with the royal food and wine, and he asked the chief official for permission not to defile himself this way" (Dan. 1:8 NIV).

The King James Version says Daniel "purposed in his heart"; some other translations render it as he "determined"; the Good News Bible says he "made up his mind." All these versions are instructive in letting us know where consecration starts. It starts with a purposeful determination in our minds not to defile ourselves.

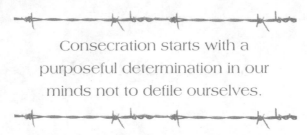

Consecration starts with a
purposeful determination in our
minds not to defile ourselves.

Consecrate means "to dedicate, to sanctify, or to keep holy." Daniel's decision not to defile himself was a decision to consecrate himself or to keep himself holy. Consecration is never done without an object or purpose. A thing or a person is consecrated or kept holy for another person's use. In other words, consecration involves keeping a person or thing in a state fit for another's use. When a person is consecrated to another, the consecrated party makes sure that there is nothing that will prevent him or her from being fit and available for the other's use.

LOVE COMPELS US TO A CONSECRATED LIFE

What could drive us to the point where we are willing to do or not to do something in order to remain fit and pleasing to another? It is answered in one word: love. The love of God is what compels us to live a consecrated life.

Love is developed in the place of intimacy and relationship. The more time you spend with someone, the greater the likelihood that your heart will be drawn toward that person. We need to understand that one of the greatest motivations we can develop to live a life of purity, holiness, and consecration is to allow our hearts to overflow with love toward God.

Jesus said, "If ye love Me, keep My commandments" (John 14:15). This Scripture has often been interpreted to mean that keeping God's commands is proof of our love for Him. I do believe there is validity in this interpretation because truly one of the ways we prove our love for God is by keeping His commands. But I want us to look at this Scripture from another perspective.

Those of you who are married or who have been in love with someone will understand this perspective. When you met your wife-to-be or when you fell in love with someone, you were willing to do so much for that person. You listened carefully to find out what that person liked or disliked, you found out the person's interests, and you did things for that person. When most men meet a woman and fall in love, they are ready to do almost anything (within godly boundaries) that they know the woman likes or wants them to do. Do they do these things to prove they love the woman? Yes, but more than to just prove their love, they do such things because they love her!

I am simply saying, when we truly love a person, the love in our hearts makes us do what will please the one we love. We do not want to offend, and we conduct ourselves in a manner that will foster the relationship with that person.

When we love God, we will obey His commandments. Our love for Him will compel us to obey Him. That love will drive us to a life of consecration, a life where we are fit for intimacy with Him.

Our love for God is balanced with the fear of God. Many people claim to love Him, but their actions demonstrate a lack of the fear of the Lord. Love for God must be balanced with the fear of God. That is the only way we can live a consecrated life. Jesus said, "And fear not them which kill the body, but are not able to kill the soul: but rather fear Him which is able to destroy both soul and body in hell" (Matt. 10:28).

WE ARE CALLED TO BE SET APART

Daniel determined not to defile himself. He wanted to remain a person the Master could relate with and speak to at anytime. Daniel recognized that God has standards, and he knew God sticks to His standards. Some Christians think the situation or circumstances determine the standards God keeps; if everyone is lying, cheating, and cutting corners to get what they want—if that's the norm in the society I live in— then God knows it's okay to do the same once in a while. After all, "everybody is doing it."

Daniel could have thought, *I am a slave in a foreign land, but God has been faithful. He opened the door for me to serve in the king's palace. Surely He will not mind if I eat the meat and drink the wine— after all, that is what has been given to me. You know, this is Babylon, not Jerusalem! When in Rome, do as the Romans do!*

This is called situational ethics, which means the situation determines the ethics. But Daniel did not think this way. Daniel knew God sticks to His standards! His standard is and always has been His Word, the terms of the covenant.

There was nothing intrinsically wrong with the meat that the king ate and the wine he drank. The problem was that the meat and the wine were used in idol worship. That was what made it wrong for the man who was consecrated to God.

Daniel determined to be set apart from Babylon, even though he lived in Babylon. He was not ready to allow Babylon in him. We are to be in the world but not of it (see John 17:14-18). This is a vital key for Christians today who want to live victoriously behind enemy lines. There are things going on in the world that are normal and accepted by the world's standards. The question is: Whose standards will rule your life—God's or the world's?

The Bible says:

> *Be ye not unequally yoked together with unbelievers: for what fellowship hath righteousness with unrighteousness? And what communion hath light with darkness? And what concord hath Christ with Belial? Or what part hath he that believeth with an infidel? And what agreement hath the temple of God with idols? For ye are the temple of the living God; as God hath said, I will dwell in them, and walk in them; and I will be their God, and they shall be My people. Wherefore come out from among them, and be ye separate, saith the Lord, and touch not the unclean thing; and I will receive you. And will be a Father unto you, and ye shall be My sons and daughters, saith the Lord Almighty. Having therefore these promises, dearly beloved, let us cleanse ourselves from all filthiness of the flesh and spirit, perfecting holiness in the fear of God (2 Corinthians 6:14-7:1).*

God calls His people to come out and be separate. God wants us to be separated unto Him. Without a total separation there is no way we will be able to fulfill the Master's purpose and live for Him in these last days.

The enemy's strategy has been to bring the world into the Church. The present-day Church has not taken a position that will allow the sons of God to manifest. The things going on in the world have crept into the Church. The carnality we talk about in the world is now in the Church. These days, sometimes you cannot even tell the difference, except by the lingo like, "Praise the Lord." Unmarried "brothers" and "sisters" are sleeping together, and no one raises an alarm. As long as they still come to church and pay their tithe, others in the church act like everything is okay. Everyone is patting one another on the back, and it is business as usual.

God wants us to be separated unto Him. The enemy's strategy has been to bring the world into the Church.

We have failed to realize that for every sin we yield to and every defilement we allow, we are not only disobeying God, we are also losing spiritual ground. The enemy is taking spiritual territory. There are so many churches today, but the enemy still holds much territory in the spirit. The Kingdom of God is the area where we have allowed His dominion. Every sin, every compromise, every defilement and act of disobedience is a rejection of God's dominion and handing over territory to the enemy.

If we allow ourselves to be defiled, then when we face challenges we are unable to stand. Too many of us have skeletons in our cupboards. We are not sold out to God, so we have not emptied our cupboards. Daniel was a young man, but he was completely sold out to his God. He was not moved by the things around him—by the accolade or the clapping of hands—nor was he concerned about creating an impression.

We are in an age of image and impressions. Many people are trying to create an image and make an impression that will cover up for the emptiness that is in them. We would rather create an impression that everything is okay, than to bring out and expose the rotting skeletons we have hidden.

God is calling His people aside, separating them from the world, and creating a covenant mind-set in them for Kingdom exploits. God wants to elevate and promote us, and He has to prepare us for that season of promotion. The enemy may try to force us into that promotion before we are ready. If he succeeds, we will not be qualified as far as Heaven is concerned. Then instead of bringing a blessing, it will bring a curse because we did not take our place in God's timing, waiting for Him.

We are being prepared for a future in God; meanwhile, we should not be enticed in the present to be like others, to copy others, and to risk losing out on our destiny. My prayer is that God will show you His dream for you. Even though others may be eating and drinking the king's meat and wine, may you have the grace to make up your mind not to defile yourself. You might think you look foolish, but you will endure even after many have long gone. Daniel served God's purpose through the reign of at least four kings; even when the reign of some of them came to an end, Daniel continued to function as God's man in the kingdom. God gave him his rightful place.

Do not seek a position you are not internally prepared for. If you want to succeed over the long haul, wait for God and do it God's way. If you care only about the short term, then you can go for it now. God wants you to go through the process, so that you will be properly equipped for what He has prepared for you. Shortcuts do not exist in spiritual matters. What looks like a shortcut may end up being a detour that gets you side-tracked. Stay on the straight and narrow way!

CONSECRATION MEANS NOT BOWING TO SIN

Consecration today also means "not bowing to the pressures of sin." In Daniel chapter 3, we read the story of the image of gold:

> *King Nebuchadnezzar made an image of gold, ninety feet high and nine feet wide, and set it up on the plain of Dura in the province of Babylon. He then summoned the satraps, prefects, governors, advisers, treasurers, judges, magistrates and all the other provincial officials to come to the dedication of the image he had set up. So the satraps, prefects, governors, advisers, treasurers, judges, magistrates and all the other provincial officials assembled for the dedication of the image that King Nebuchadnezzar had set up, and they stood before it. Then the herald loudly proclaimed, "This is what you are commanded to do, O peoples, nations and men of every language: As soon as you hear the sound of the horn, flute, zither, lyre, harp, pipes and all kinds of music, you must fall down and worship the image of gold that King Nebuchadnezzar has set up. Whoever does not fall down and worship will immediately be thrown into a blazing furnace." Therefore, as soon as they heard the sound of the horn, flute, zither, lyre, harp and all kinds of music, all the peoples, nations and men of every language fell down and worshiped the image of gold that King Nebuchadnezzar had set up. At this time some astrologers came forward and denounced the Jews. They said to King Nebuchadnezzar, "O king, live forever! You have issued a decree, O king, that everyone who hears the sound of the horn, flute, zither, lyre, harp, pipes and all kinds of music must fall down and worship the image of gold, and that whoever does not fall down and worship will be thrown into a blazing furnace. But*

there are some Jews whom you have set over the affairs of the province of Babylon—Shadrach, Meshach and Abednego—who pay no attention to you, O king. They neither serve your gods nor worship the image of gold you have set up" (Daniel 3:1-12 NIV).

What do you think people are bowing to today: money, power, or fame? It is all out there, making demands on everyone, asking humanity to bow. Jesus faced the same temptation; satan offered Him wealth, power, all the kingdoms of the world. In exchange, satan asked for only one thing: "Bow to me" (see Matt. 4:8-9). The same offer is being made to so many Christians today.

But we need to remember that the three Hebrew children were asked to bow to an image. It is always an image. Satan perverts what God gives; he generates an image of the real thing but with a perverted purpose. He deceives people into thinking the image is the real thing. When they do bow, they realize they do not have what they thought bowing would give them. I have always said, "What you compromise to get, you are bound to lose."

A consecrated Christian will never compromise his principles or his relationship with God for what the world has to offer. This was the mind-set that the apostles had. This is why they gladly gave up their earthly goods and even their lives. They suffered beatings, persecution, and shame. They realized that everything they could see was temporal. The real substance is in God. Consecration is a lifestyle that is committed to God.

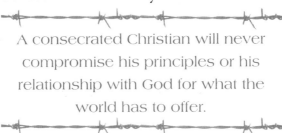

A consecrated Christian will never compromise his principles or his relationship with God for what the world has to offer.

In the Book of Esther, we read of another man who refused to bow. His name was Mordecai. "All the royal officials at the king's gate knelt down and paid honor to Haman, for the king had commanded this concerning him. But Mordecai would not kneel down or pay him honor" (Esther 3:2 NIV). Mordecai refused to bow to Haman. Haman was a proud bigot; he was full of himself and wanted worship and adoration from men. But according to Jewish tradition, one should not bow to men like that.

What does Haman represent today? Haman represents sin. Sin goes around parading itself—just like Haman—glorying in the fact that everyone is bowing to it. Sin is telling Christians to do all sorts of wrong things. Sin makes them notice other Christians who appear to be doing wrong things and getting away with it. It's telling young men and women, "Other young men and women are having premarital sex—why not you?" It's telling business people, "In business it's the ruthless and greedy—those who are not afraid to do anything—who get ahead. So what are you going to do?"

WE MUST BE PREPARED FOR AND EXPECT TO FACE FIRE

Sin has been going around saying, "Bow, bow, bow the knee; bow the knee to me." Are there Christians who are ready to say, "I will not bow," today? Listen, anytime we say, "I will not bow," we should get ready for the fire. God will watch as we enter the fire. But I've got news—the fire will not have power over us.

I am writing to a generation. A generation of people who have made up their minds not to bow. A generation of people who have made up their minds not to defile themselves. A generation who is saying, "We will not bow," even if it means going into the fire! A generation who values a God-connection above anything that the world has to offer.

We should not tell people, "If you do not bow, then you will not go through the fire." This is not true. We may go through the fire, but it will have no power over us. As it says in Isaiah:

> *When you pass through the waters, I will be with you; and when you pass through the rivers, they will not sweep over you. When you walk through the fire, you will not be burned; the flames will not set you ablaze* (Isaiah 43:2 NIV).

This Scripture does not say that we will not enter the fire, but it does say that when we walk through the fire we will come out unscathed.

Whenever we decide to take a stand against the devil, whenever we decide we will not bow, the enemy may bombard our minds with negative thoughts. The devil might tell us, "If you don't tell lies, if you don't cheat, if you don't pretend to be who you are not, you'll never make it." The devil is trying to tell us at such times, "I will sentence you to the fire of misery, mediocrity, and poverty." We must know how to reply to the devil. We must be able to tell him, "I am not slow to answer you—I will not bow!"

When we take a stand for righteousness, integrity, and truth, we cannot lose. The very things we refuse to bow to, will bow to us when we come out of the fire. The Hebrew children had made their decision before the question was asked.

This is the secret: When we do not bow, what we refuse to bow to will bow to us. When we bow, we lose it. We lose it because what we bow to will control us. We will not use it for what God wants. It will use us for what it wants.

This is why many people today, lack proper direction for their lives. Instead of responding to God and His purposes, they respond to money and its demands. Jesus was very clear when He said, "You cannot serve both God and Money" (Matt. 6:24 NIV). In bowing to money and to the things of the world, we lose our freedom. People often ask me why I look so calm and free. It is simple really; I do not bow because I am ready to go through the fire.

We should not think that we will be celebrated when we refuse to bow. I am not talking about not being celebrated by the world; nobody should expect that really. I am saying that we should not expect to be celebrated by our brothers and sisters in the Church.

Do you think the other Jews celebrated when Shadrach, Meshach, and Abednego refused to bow? Do you think their eventual promotion was celebrated? No! I believe that the other Jews envied them and hated them because they (the other Jews) had already bowed. They probably were angry with those three because they represented a race that did not bow and excelled because they refused to bow. In the same way, we should not expect applause when we refuse to bow. We should not expect accolades when the resultant promotion comes. All the same, we should not bow!

THE TIME TO PREPARE IS BEFORE WE ARE IN THE FIRE

We must make up our minds not to defile ourselves! Living for God means living a consecrated life, living according to

His standard. The story of Daniel and his friends teaches us that if we are not able to make such decisions when the pressure is less intense, then it is unlikely that we will be able to stand in the day of trial. If we cannot make such decisions in simple matters (like consuming meat and wine in Daniel's case), then we will be unlikely to make the decision when facing the fire. We should decide to live a consecrated life now, not when we are staring at the burning flames.

When such decisions are not made, we give the devil room to lead us off course. It is at such times, that we are likely to hear some "wise sayings." We may begin to hear statements like, "Let's be wise," or "I am bowing on the outside, but inside I am standing." This is why God does not get the credit for most of our "success." We have become a generation who lacks the backbone to pay the price to know Him. We lack the backbone to stand for Him and see God demonstrate His glory in our time. But there is a generation! I prophesy that there is a generation that has a backbone—a backbone reinforced with the power of God, which will not bow to sin. This generation will win with righteousness; I call on the Mordecais to stand up!

Mordecai did not bow to Haman, and the very gallows that Haman had prepared for Mordecai were used to destroy Haman (see Esther 5:14; 7:9-10). In the same way, the fire killed those who threw the Hebrew children into the fire, but it did not harm the three Hebrew children (see Dan. 3:22-27). There was a clear distinction in the minds of the three that they did not belong to Babylon. So, when Babylon brought its threat, it was really no threat to them.

The Bible tells us not to "fear their fears" (see Isa. 8:12). At times, we have compromised so much with the world that we are no longer separate from the world. Yet, we wonder why we are not separate from the world when calamities come upon the world.

In Matthew chapter 5, Jesus says that as believers we are to be the salt of the earth and the light of the world (see Matt. 5:13-14). One thing about light and darkness is that they do not mix. Jesus specifically used light when referring to our relationship with the world. *World* here is the translation of the Greek word *kosmos*, which is the word used when referring to "the systems or arrangements of the world." As far as the systems of the world are concerned, we are to see ourselves as light—distinct and separate from the world.

Today, many Christians have one foot in the church and one foot outside in the world. We are not separate. In order for us to be able to overcome the Babylonian systems, we must have the mind-set of a people separated from the world and separated unto God. No matter how hard you try, you cannot get light and darkness to mix. There is definitely a place for us to reach out to people bound by the world—just like Jesus did—but we must not allow the systems governing such people to influence our thoughts, attitudes, or actions. This is why Jesus also refers to believers as salt. Even though salt seems to mix with the environment in which it is placed, the mixing allows the salt to influence its environment and not vice versa.

One of the reasons the world has been able to infiltrate the Church so well, is because our values have become so much like the world's values. We sometimes celebrate the rich as though they are closer to God because they are rich. Mammon seems to have taken the place of Christ in His Church.

We must be a generation who will say no to religious activities that are without God. We must hate such religion and the worldly mind-set that is trying to take over the Church. There must be a dethroning of anti-Christ attitudes in the Church. In some places, politics have mixed with religion, and there are those who are bowing to sin, bowing to mammon; we must not be part of this.

GRACE WILL GIVE US THE STRENGTH WE NEED

Looking back at the story of Daniel and his three friends, we see that these three Hebrew children had received grace to say no to sin, to say no to compromise. For most believers, grace is a big cover-up. We live a life of sin and say, "Thank God for His grace." Grace is not a cover-up for our sins. Grace is not an excuse for our weaknesses.

God's grace imparts a dimension into our spirit that enables us to say no to sin. The Book of Titus says, "For the grace of God that brings salvation has appeared to all men" (Titus 2:11 NIV). Grace is taking a position, a permanent position of having said no to sin. Then when we are presented with an opportunity to sin, when sin is offered on a platter of gold, we must remember that grace has taught us to say no! Sin will no longer be an option.

No matter how hungry you are, even if you are starving, I do not think that you would be tempted to eat sand. Not even the beautiful white sand on the beach. Why would it not be a temptation? Because you are in a state of having said no to eating sand. You know sand is not meant for eating, and you are aware that there would be a negative effect in your body if you ate it. What would you think of someone who offered you sand to eat? One thing is certain; you would not consider such a person a friend.

Grace enables us to see sin for what it really is. No matter how well packaged or dressed sin may be, it was not meant for us and will definitely have negative effects on our spirit, soul, and body. How about the persons who offer us sin? Why do we still sometimes find it so easy to commune with people who are offering us a deadly substance? Surely, such people—no matter who or what they are to us naturally—are not our friends.

Grace enables us to see sin for what it really is. No matter how well packaged or dressed sin may be, it was not meant for us and will definitely have negative effects on our spirit, soul, and body.

Grace will give us the backbone to say no to sin. It will no longer be a debate; it will no longer be an issue. We must enter this dimension of grace. The three Hebrew children were operating in this dimension, which is why they could boldly say, "We do not need to defend ourselves before you in this matter" (Dan. 3:16 NIV). They had taken a stand; they had made their decision.

I think it should be very clear to us now that it takes grace to live a consecrated life. Living a consecrated life is not a life of following rules and regulations. It is a life of having received grace. The grace of God is available to all who are saved (see Titus 2:11-12). In describing John and Jesus, the Bible says that "He himself [John] was not the light; he came only as a witness to the light" (John 1:8 NIV). The Bible states clearly that it is from the fullness of Jesus that we receive grace (see John 1:16). The law came by Moses, but grace and truth came by Jesus. He gives us grace, so that we can live by the truth He reveals to us.

Let us make it our prayer for God to bring us into this level of grace, this level of having said no to sin. What was Daniel's greatest asset? I believe that it was his consecration to God, his separation to God, and his level of satisfaction in God. He lived the example of a crucified life; he lived holy unto the Lord and in the fear of God. All this is revealed in the Book of Daniel where it says, "But Daniel purposed in his heart…" (Dan. 1:8). This verse highlights his consecration to God, and this was a consecration he wisely maintained, without exposing himself as a rebel in the king's court. May God give us the grace to live a consecrated life.

BEWARE OF THE DANGER OF KEEPING OFFENSES

What about offenses? Many people are defiled simply because they refuse to be doers of the Word. God's Word says we should forgive (see Matt. 6:12; Mark 11:25-26). If we refuse to forgive when we have been offended, then we open the door to bitterness and bitterness defiles (see Heb. 12:15).

A study of Hebrews chapter 12 shows that offenses born out of correction can lead to defilement. We are advised to look "diligently lest any man fail of the grace of God; lest any root of bitterness springing up trouble you, and thereby many be defiled; lest there be any fornicator, or profane person, as Esau…"

(Heb. 12:15-16). These verses indicate that bitterness, which is a product of unforgiveness, can be a root cause of defilement.

This chapter of Hebrews encourages us to embrace correction from God and then goes on to say that we should "follow peace with all men, and holiness, without which no man shall see the Lord" (see Heb. 12:5-7;14). To *see the Lord* means we are to "experience His presence in our everyday living."

I believe that if Joseph had allowed bitterness against his brothers to enter his heart, he would not have been in a position of grace to say no to Potiphar's wife. The Bible says that the Lord was with Joseph (see Gen. 39:2,21). He cultivated an intimacy with God through his love and fear of God. This intimacy released grace to forgive his brothers as God showed him His (God's) perspective of his experience (see Gen. 45:3-14).

Offenses can affect the state of our hearts. Our receptivity to the things of God can be affected or polluted, opening the door of our hearts to impurities that can defile in many ways.

We have looked at what it means to be consecrated and to live a consecrated life. Consecration is essential to a relationship with God and to being equipped to fulfill our destiny. But what about relationships with others, especially with those in authority? This will be the topic of discussion in our next chapter.

CHAPTER ONE—HIGHLIGHTS AND WISDOM

- Daniel's greatest asset was his consecration to God. Consecration starts with a purposeful determination in our minds not to defile ourselves.

- God always sticks to His standard, and His standard is His Word—the terms of His covenant.

- Daniel determined to separate himself from Babylon. Although he lived in Babylon, he didn't allow Babylon within him. We are to be in the world, but not of the world. Separation is not the same as isolation.

- Without a total heart separation there is no way we will be able to fulfill the Master's purpose and live for Him in these days.

- For every sin we yield to, for every defilement we allow, we are not only disobeying God, we are losing spiritual ground.

- While we are being prepared for a future in God, we should not be enticed in the present to be like others, to copy others, and to risk losing out on our destiny.

- If we want to succeed over the long haul, we must wait for God and do it God's way; if we care only about the short term, then we can go for it now. We should not seek a position that we are not internally prepared for.

- Every time we say, "I will not bow," we should get ready for the fire! God will watch us as we enter the fire; the fire will not have power over us.

- Living a consecrated life is not living a life of following rules and regulations. It is a life of having received grace. The grace of God is available to all who are saved.

- We must watch out for offenses in our lives. We should not be hasty to be judgmental or unnecessarily critical. We should keep ourselves in the love of God.

Relationships With Those in Authority

Submission is one of the principles of victory that focuses on our relationship with man.

Unlike many Christians in the Church today, Daniel knew how to relate with men, particularly in the context of those in authority over him. For most of us, working with a "heathen" or unsaved boss is a great challenge. Somewhere lodged deep within us is a mentality that says, "For the rod of the wicked shall not rest upon the lot of the righteous" (Ps. 125:3).

Other Scriptures have also played a major role in influencing our relationships with those in authority over us. In Deuteronomy it says, "And the Lord will make you the head and not the tail; you shall be above only, and not be beneath..." (Deut. 28:13 NKJV). Some of us have interpreted such Scriptures to imply that unbelievers are not supposed to have authority over believers in any context at all.

Even Christians who work with a boss or authorities who are Christians or saved, still sometimes have problems dealing with the question of how to relate to those whom God has placed in authority over them. As innocent as it may seem, the question of who has authority over us and how we relate to them, is a key determinant in our ability to walk in victory in these times.

The question of who has authority
over us and how we relate to them
is a key determinant in our ability to
walk in victory in these times.

TO WHOM SHOULD WE SUBMIT?

According to *Merriam-Webster's Collegiate Dictionary*, to *submit* means "to yield to governance or authority; to yield oneself to the authority or will of another; to surrender; to permit oneself to be subjected to something."

It says in the Book of Romans, "Let every person be subject to the governing authorities. For there is no authority except from God, and the authorities that exist have been instituted by God" (Rom. 13:1 The Common Edition: New Testament 1865). The Analytical-Literal Translation of this verse is, "Let every soul be submitting to higher [or, governing] authorities, for [there] is no authority except from God, but the existing authorities have been appointed by God" (Rom. 13:1 ALT). From this verse, it is clear that God expects us to submit to the higher or governing authorities because according to His Word, He places them over us.

In his book, *Under Cover,* John Bevere states:

> First, who are these "governing authorities"? In this specific text Paul referred to civil or governmental authorities. However, these words of exhortation apply not only to governmental leaders but also encompass other areas of delegated authority. What we glean from this text should be applied to all areas of delegated authority. The New Testament speaks of four divisions of delegated authority: civil, church, family, and social....[1]

God expects us to yield our will to those He has placed in authority over us. This speaks not only of our actions but also of our attitude toward those in authority over us.

WHAT DOES IT MEAN TO SUBMIT?

To *submit* implies "to surrender." God, in His wisdom, has chosen that the key to winning is surrendering! This is why submission is so difficult for many of us. We often surrender only when we can no longer fight or resist. Very rarely do we surrender by choice. Yet, to be victorious God says that we must surrender.

In the Book of Luke it says, "And Jesus increased in wisdom and stature, and in favour with God and man" (Luke 2:52). Here the Bible clearly states that Jesus, among other things, grew in favor with God and man. As long as we are on earth, we must realize that our ability to relate to others will influence the level of success we will be able to attain.

Let us look again at Daniel chapter 1 where it says, "But Daniel was determined not to defile himself by eating the food and wine given to them by the king. He asked the chief of staff for permission not to eat these unacceptable foods" (Dan. 1:8 NLT). Notice that Daniel had made up his mind about what he was going to do (or rather, what he was not going to do), but there was a little problem. Daniel and his friends had been placed in the care of the king's "master of his eunuchs" (see Dan. 1:3). Because they were under this master's care, the master was responsible for what Daniel and his friends ate or did not eat. In this situation, Daniel did not have the authority to decide his diet. What did Daniel do?

The Bible says that Daniel "asked the chief official for permission not to defile himself this way" (Dan. 1:8 NIV). There are many people today who desire something from those in authority over them, or who want to talk to those God has placed over them, but they do not have the attitude that Daniel had. Daniel not only understood the role of authority, but he also understood the importance of attitude as it relates to the principle of submission.

THE IMPORTANCE OF HAVING A RIGHT ATTITUDE WHEN SUBMITTING

Submission is one of the key principles that will enable us live victoriously and overcome in the times in which we live. It is important to remember that submission is, first of all, an attitude. Submission is primarily revealed in the attitude of our hearts toward those God has placed over us. In Romans chapter 13 it says:

> *Everyone must submit himself to the governing authorities, for there is no authority except that which God has established.*

The authorities that exist have been established by God. Consequently, he who rebels against the authority is rebelling against what God has instituted, and those who do so will bring judgment on themselves (Romans 13:1-2 NIV).

The Bible clearly tells us to be subject to higher powers. The Word of God also makes it very clear that all authorities are ordained of God. As believers we must understand that having a right attitude toward those in authority is not optional behavior.

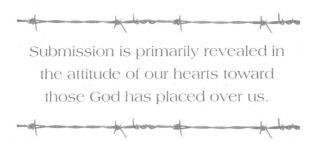

Submission is primarily revealed in the attitude of our hearts toward those God has placed over us.

Daniel knew this. This is why Daniel consistently maintained the right attitude of submission, even though those in authority over him were heathen rulers with no covenant or relationship with God. Daniel beseeched the authority God had placed over him. He maintained a submissive attitude; he was not arrogant or rude in making his request. He said, "Please test me for ten days" (see Dan. 1:12 NIV). He had a submissive attitude even though he had great skill and knowledge.

I see many of my colleagues—my contemporaries and even some younger than me—who have much knowledge and great skill in spiritual things, but they do not know how to conduct themselves with wisdom, so their great knowledge and skill rarely bring significant promotion. A number of them have allowed their great knowledge and skill to puff them up, so much that they exalt themselves in their hearts above the leaders under whom God has placed them. Outwardly, they may appear humble and respectful, but inwardly, they despise and look down on those whom God has placed in authority over them.

Daniel and his friends never fell into this trap. At times, God deliberately places us under leaders who have glaring faults or who may be outright wicked people. God does this to test our hearts, to see whether we are willing to submit to those whom He has placed over us. He wants to know whether we will submit only when the going is good, or whether we are willing to be obedient to His Word at all times. Even when the faults of another person are blatantly evident to us, are we willing to respect and submit to the authority that God has given to such a person?

We see another good example of the submissive attitude embraced by Daniel and his friends in chapter 3 of the Book of Daniel. Here we read that King Nebuchadnezzar had made an image of gold, and all men were commanded to bow down to this image at the blowing of a trumpet. This instruction was clearly contrary to the commands of God. Shadrach, Meshach, and Abednego knew that as covenant children, they were forbidden by God to bow down or worship any image or idol. They were in a situation where the authority that God had brought them under, had given a directive contrary to God's commands. Of course, obeying the king and disobeying God was out of the question, but how did these Hebrew children handle the situation?

> *Shadrach, Meshach and Abednego replied to the king, "O Nebuchadnezzar, we do not need to defend ourselves before you in this matter. If we are thrown into the blazing furnace, the God we serve is able to save us from it, and He will rescue us from*

your hand, O king. But even if He does not, we want you to know, O king, that we will not serve your gods or worship the image of gold you have set up" (Daniel 3:16-18 NIV).

This was their reply to the king's command. If you read it carefully, you will see that even while refusing to obey the king's command, they maintained an attitude of respect for the king. They did not scold or abuse him; they respectfully told the king that they were not going to bow. They had respect for the office of the king as well as for the king himself.

Our ability to embrace the principle of submission may make the difference in whether we will be able to fulfill our destiny in God or not. We must remember that even though we are not *of* the world, we are in the world, and there are principles that God has given to us, which are specifically designed to help us with our relationships with other people in the world.

Many Christians are suffering and failing in life, not as a result of persecution stirred up against them by the devil, but simply because they have failed to employ godly principles in their relationships with their fellow man. Submission is one of the principles of victory that focuses on our relationship with man.

THE EXAMPLE OF DAVID AND SAUL

David is another person who understood and embraced the principle of submission. Some background information will help us to see clearly what life was like for David. If you remember his story, you probably recall that when Samuel anointed David to be king, "the Spirit of the Lord came upon David" (1 Sam. 16:13 NIV).

In the next verse it says, "Now the Spirit of the Lord had departed from Saul, and an evil spirit from the Lord tormented him" (1 Sam. 16:14 NIV). It is interesting to note that as David was moving on the path of fulfilling his destiny, God had him serve under Saul—a man whom the Spirit of the Lord had left, and upon whom a demonic or evil spirit had come.

Naturally, we would conclude that Saul would be a bad leader to serve under. That's obvious, isn't it? If a man is tormented and influenced by an evil spirit, the probability that his decisions will be almost totally influenced by that evil spirit is very high. Indeed, reading through the story of Saul's life, we see evidence of evil behavior being exhibited many times. For instance, Saul ordered many priests and the inhabitants of an entire city to be killed (see 1 Sam. 22:17-19 NIV). He repeatedly tried to kill David without just cause, and he did many other terrible things.

Throughout this time when Saul was doing horrible things, we have no record of David ever criticizing, complaining, or grumbling against Saul. David maintained a reverent attitude toward Saul throughout Saul's lifetime. Even when David had an opportunity to rebel or to take revenge, he did not. He consistently recognized the authority of God upon Saul, regardless of Saul's evil behavior; David remained submissive.

Although David had been anointed to be king, he was not yet king. While Saul was still king, David behaved wisely toward the men in Saul's armies. Though David had been anointed, he knew the time had not yet come for him to be king. He recognized that there was a king—an authority over him—and he stayed in submission to that authority. David conducted himself according to the context of God's will for his time.

From the story of David, we learn that there is a way we ought to conduct ourselves in submission to authority and in humility, which is in resonance with the season of life we are in. We clearly see that to submit to those in authority over us, is to honor God by respecting the authority He has given to those over us. True submission is to recognize God's authority on the people occupying positions of authority over us, and to accord heart respect to them because of their God-given authority.

We need to maintain a heart of honor and respect for those in authority over us even when they have missed God. There are the stories of Samuel and Eli in First Samuel chapter 3; of Daniel in Daniel chapter 6, even when the king ordered the people to pray to no other god; and of the three young Hebrew men who were commanded to bow to the golden image in Daniel chapter 3. Our hearts should first be in submission to God. He is the ultimate authority, and all authority flows from Him; we then should also submit to His authority-delegate in our lives. Whether it be parents, church leaders, or civil leaders, they all deserve our heart submission, where seeds of pride can never be allowed to take root. Our attitude of submission then determines the response of God to our situations.

To submit to those in authority over us, is to honor God by respecting the authority He has given to those over us.

IT IS GOD WHO PLACES US UNDER SPIRITUAL AUTHORITY

We should also submit to the spiritual authority that God establishes in our lives. Most of the time, God places us under spiritual authority according to His purpose and destiny for our lives. What does this mean? It means that we do not necessarily choose whom God will place in authority over us spiritually. You may be able to choose who your boss in the office will be (by choosing where you work). You may be able to choose which political or government authority will be over you (by choosing where you live). You may even be able to choose which man will have authority over you individually (by choosing who you marry). In all these choices, wise people allow God to lead them; but most importantly we need to let God lead us to who the spiritual authority in our lives will be.

God, through Jesus Christ, has positioned ministry gifts in the Body of Christ, in general; and He places or sets each one of us under the authority of the head of a local assembly, in particular. We should choose which church to attend as guided by God. We should allow God to lead each one of us to the church He has chosen for us. Once we are in a church, God expects us to submit to the authority He has placed over that church. It is as we submit and are faithful, that we will see manifestations of the fulfillment of destiny and purpose.

God in His wisdom has chosen that we all should operate through families. As it says in the Book of Psalms, "God sets the solitary in families" (Ps. 68:6 NKJV). In the Kingdom, our immediate family is the local assembly where God has placed us. Just as we are to submit to our father in our natural homes, we are expected to submit to those He places over the local assembly.

In Revelation chapters 2 and 3, God had messages that He wanted to pass on to the churches. But in speaking to the churches, He did not call everyone that was a member and talk to them all. He identified the leader—the angel or messenger—and gave the message to that angel (see Rev. 2:1 NIV).

Only those who are submitted to their leader will be able to hear the voice of God in the voice of their leader. This is why submission is so important! Often, God speaks to us through the leaders whom He has set in authority over us. If we choose to despise and disregard them, we will never hear the voice of God through them.

God must be first in our lives, no doubt about that at all, but the godly authority placed over us must be respected. A humble person will be taught by the anointing and will get the balance. Godly authority is always confirmed in the hearts of godly people. If a person who is under God's authority speaks God's word to you, there will be a witness in your heart that the word is of God.

We must understand that God ordained the principle of submission to authority, and He will not break it. We must allow God to be placed first in our lives and respect everything He has put in place. We must strive to follow God's order and not our own way. It is only when we do things His way that we can be sure of always walking in victory.

SUBMISSION PREPARES US TO FULFILL OUR CALL AND PURPOSE

Daniel and his friends understood that there was much more to submission than just being respectful. Submission is a powerful tool that God uses to put us in a position where He can get us ready for His calling and purposes. To obey a calling means to be willing to go through tutelage and submit ourselves, just like Jesus (who is our pattern) did, so that our gifts and calling can be developed in a safe environment of submission. It is only then that our gift and calling can be presented to humanity and be a blessing.

Many of us fail to recognize that spiritual authority has been given to us as a covering in the spirit. Instead of waiting in a place of submission, we may jump out and try to "make things happen." In a bid to make things happen, we may step out before the right time and suffer disastrous consequences as a result.

When we submit to spiritual authority, God covers or hides us to mature and train us. This is a period of growth and development. When we do not allow this process to take place, we do not mature in the spirit, and we become vulnerable. For example, when a baby is born, that baby is vulnerable. A baby is cared for by a family and kept in a home. No caring person has a baby and then throws the baby outside, exposing the baby to the natural elements. If that happens, the baby will likely die. The baby dies not because the natural elements are bad, but because the baby was exposed too soon.

In a similar way, God places us under spiritual authority to prevent premature exposure. God hides us; He shuts us up and He shuts us in. Why does He do this? He does this to mature and train us. Who does He use to nurture and train us? He uses those He has placed in authority over us.

The person might not even be a Christian! God, who knows the purpose and calling He has for us, knows the best people to use to train us. It may be that teacher in your school whom you dislike so much, perhaps your boss in the office—I mean the one who is always criticizing everything you do! It may even be the father or mother you always felt never understood you!

God has a purpose for every authority He has allowed in your life. It is up to you to have enough faith and trust in God to believe the Scripture that says, "…there is no authority except that which God has established. The authorities that exist have been established by God" (Rom. 13:1 NIV). Because God has allowed that person to have authority in your life, the best thing you can do is to stay in submission.

God hides us in a church; He hides us in a home in a family; He hides us in an office under a boss; He hides us under spiritual authority to mature and train us—until we are ready for the assignment He has destined us to fulfill.

He hides us under spiritual authority to mature and train us, until we are ready for the assignment He has destined us to fulfill.

THE EXAMPLE OF MOSES

The Bible says that when Moses was born, his mother hid him for three months. When she could no longer hide him, she placed him in a basket along the riverbank (see Exod. 2:1-3). Note that it was not Moses who decided he was too big for the place where God had first kept him. God by His Spirit, revealed it to the authority (his parents), and they knew it was time for Moses to move on. Although they did not know where he was supposed to go, they knew enough to get him on the way to the next place where God wanted to hide him. God will always give the authorities over your life enough information to make the right move for the next phase of your life that you need to enter.

God arranged for Pharaoh's daughter to find Moses and "hide" him for another 40 years. God chose to hide him under the authority of a person who had been very cruel to the Is-raelites because that was the best place, at that time, to get the training and development necessary for God's calling for him.

But Moses stepped out of the covering of that authority prematurely and killed a man. I know this because Moses had to run for his life! (See Exodus 2:11-15.) He was running from the same authority he had lived under for 40 years. If Moses had killed that man while in submission to authority, he would not have needed to run. He was in rebellion by that action and he knew it, which is why he ran away.

Whenever we are not in submission to authority, either in our words or by our actions, we know it. That is why many Christians are running today—running from church to church, from conference to conference, from meeting to meeting. So many Christians are running from the authority that God has placed them under and used to train them for many years. Like Moses, they have an idea of God's calling on their lives. But in-stead of staying under the authority and allowing God to tell them when to move, they take matters into their own hands and end up running.

Have you ever wondered why God needed to get Pharaoh to give the Israelites permission to leave Egypt? He is God, is He not? He could have wiped out Pharaoh and his army with one wave of His hand. Or He could have caused Pharaoh, his armies, and the Egyptians to fall into a deep sleep for three days, while the Israelites escaped. Couldn't He have? Sure He could have!

However, God works by principles, and He does not break His Word. Pharaoh had legitimate authority over the Israelites. They had come willingly into Egypt during Joseph's lifetime and submitted themselves and their families to Pharaoh's authority. Although it is true that Pharaoh abused his authority as a steward, God had committed the Israelites to Pharaoh, for Pharaoh to watch over as a steward for Him. The very thing that Pharaoh was meant to keep and use for God, he began to abuse and use for himself. Stewardship is another worthwhile subject, but I will write about that in another book!

Because Pharaoh was a legitimate authority that God had placed over the Israelites, God needed to get that authority (Pharaoh) to release His people. That is why Moses said to Pharaoh, "…the God of Israel, says: 'Let My people go!'" (See Exodus 5:1 NIV.) Moses was saying, "You are the authority God placed over these people; now release them."

MOSES LEARNS THE IMPORTANCE OF SUBMITTING TO AUTHORITY

Let's back up in the story, and revisit when Moses ran because he did not stay under Pharaoh's authority where he had been placed. What did God do next? God placed Moses under the authority of Jethro, a priest of Midian, for another 40 years (see Exod. 3:1). Did you notice that Moses was under the authority of "unbelievers": Pharaoh, an Egyptian; and Jethro, a Midianite priest?

I believe that during this second period of 40 years, Moses really came to understand the place and importance of submission to authority. Moses came to an understanding that you don't just "jump out" because you believe God is leading or calling you. I believe Moses came to realize that God does not negotiate or compromise on His principle of submission to authority. No matter how "ungodly" the authority that God has placed you under may appear, God reckons with that person as far as your life and destiny is concerned.

God appeared to Moses while he was taking care of Jethro's flock (see Exod. 3:1). Moses was going about the business of the authority whom God had placed him under, when God appeared to him. Question: Whose business are you about? Moses saw signs and wonders, heard the voice of God, and knew without doubt that God had spoken to him. His rod even turned into a snake! Then what did Moses do?

> And Moses went and returned to Jethro his father in law, and said unto him, Let me go, I pray thee, and return unto my brethren which are in Egypt, and see whether they be yet alive. And Jethro said to Moses, Go in peace. And the Lord said unto Moses in Midian, Go, return into Egypt: for all the men are dead which sought thy life. And Moses took his wife and his sons, and set them upon an ass, and he returned to the land of Egypt: and Moses took the rod of God in his hand (Exodus 4:18-20).

Moses had learned his lesson! He knew that he needed to submit to authority and be released by those whom God had placed over him. He met Jethro and asked Jethro to release him. And Jethro did! The next thing that happened was that God spoke to Moses again!

My prayer is that you catch the importance of submission to authority. Many, who are called of God in this generation, are running when they should be hiding—hiding in the place of submission and learning from those whom God has placed over them.

Moses shouldn't have needed to run from the Egyptians, but because he was no longer under authority, he had to flee. Moses was one man when he ran away; he was a different man when he returned 40 years later. What was the difference? He came back 40 years later as a man under authority, and as a result, he had the grace to confront Pharaoh and to do God's will.

Many things hindering the people of God today are taking advantage of our rebellion. Moses never knew fear, lack, or sensed failure while he was behind enemy lines, until he stepped out from under his covering. God wants us to win, even in these perilous times. That is why He has chosen to cover us and to set people in authority over us—to protect and watch over the gifts and calling in our lives.

Many, who are called of God in this generation,
are running when they should be hiding—
hiding in the place of submission and learning
from those whom God has placed over them.

SUBMISSION MEANS RECOGNIZING THE PLACE AND POSITION OF OTHERS

We need to understand that submission to authority is not merely about saying yes to those whom God has set in authority over us. Submission is more than just an act of obedience! Especially in the current move of God, we have to recognize that submission includes our ability to recognize the place and positioning of other gifts in the Body of Christ. We must recognize their place in our lives, especially in connection to the work God has assigned to us. We must be willing to submit our gifts to others, and to recognize that it is only in the place of submission to one another that the Body of Christ can come to a place of maturity and strength.

A clear example of this can be seen in Acts chapter 8:

> *Then Philip went down to the city of Samaria, and preached Christ unto them. And the people with one accord gave heed unto those things which Philip spake, hearing and seeing the miracles which he did. For unclean spirits, crying with loud voice, came out of many that were possessed with them: and many taken with palsies, and that were lame, were healed. And there was great joy in that city. But there was a certain man, called Simon, which beforetime in the same city used sorcery, and bewitched the people of Samaria, giving out that himself was some great one: To whom they all gave heed, from the least to the greatest, saying, This man is the great power of God. And to him they had regard, because that of long time he had bewitched them with sorceries. But when they believed Philip preaching the things concerning the kingdom of God, and the name of Jesus Christ, they were baptized, both men and women. Then Simon himself believed also: and when he was baptized, he continued with Philip, and wondered, beholding the miracles and signs which were done. Now when the apostles which were at Jerusalem heard that Samaria had received the word of God, they sent unto them Peter and John: Who, when they were come down, prayed for them, that they might receive the Holy Ghost: (For as yet He was fallen upon none of them: only they were baptized in the name of the Lord Jesus.) Then laid they their hands on them, and they received the Holy Ghost* (Acts 8:5-17).

One of the weapons the enemy has used against us is to create a territorial mentality in the minds of some church leaders. Some leaders see the work that God is doing through them as their "own turf." Input from others is resisted and other giftings are not allowed to be expressed. This deception is prevalent among some leaders who think they do not have to submit to anyone. This is a high level of deception, and the devil has effectively used this weapon to cripple otherwise vibrant and active work that God intended to perform.

It is important to remember that even Jesus Christ our Lord (and pattern) lived a life of continued submission to the Father. In many places in the Scriptures, Jesus spoke of His inability to do, say, or go anywhere except what He saw or heard His Father do (see John 5:19,30; 6:38). Jesus demonstrated a life of submission unparalleled to anything we can imagine today.

Ephesians tells us to submit to one another in the fear of God (see Eph. 5:21). The commandment here leaves no one out. Submission is not meant for followers only! We all are commanded to submit to one another in the fear of God.

Compared to Jesus, none of us have the level of revelation or the power that was available to Him. Even so, Jesus was (and still is) able to submit to a higher authority. Jesus demonstrated this grace of submission from childhood. In Luke chapter 2, we read the story of how Jesus was left behind in Jerusalem (see Luke 2:41-52). A careful reading of this account reveals some important points. First, we see that Jesus knew who He was and who His Father was. Second, He knew what His Father's business was. Jesus had a clear revelation of His identity and His calling. Despite this revelation, Jesus submitted Himself to the natural authority God had placed over Him—His parents.

Jesus did not step into ministry before the right time! Oh, how I wish my generation would catch this. Many times, we have an encounter with God, we get a revelation of what He has called us to do, and then we take off! We sever the relationships that He has placed over us because in our minds, we think we can do it on our own. We allow the revelation of our identity and calling to fuel our pride, and in our hearts we exalt ourselves over those to whom God has called us to submit right now.

Submission is a Kingdom principle that applies to all in the Kingdom. Our emphasis in this chapter is with respect to those under authority for the sake of covering and protection.

Jesus provides us with a clear example of how we are to relate to those in authority and what it means to submit. In the Book of Luke, we read the story of Jesus submitting to the spiritual authority of John the Baptist in baptism. Then He submits to the leadership of the Holy Spirit and goes into the wilderness. (See Luke chapters 3 and 4.) We see Him moving from one level of submission to another. Indeed He humbled Himself and became obedient even to death on a cross (see Phil. 2:8). That was the level of His submission to His Father's will; He lived this way to show us the pattern and to demonstrate what is expected from us, too.

Understanding these concepts is critical if we are to walk in victory. Another vital component is understanding what the knowledge of God encompasses and how it equips us. This is what we will look at in the next two chapters.

ENDNOTE

1. John Bevere, *Under Cover* (Nashville, TN: Thomas Nelson, 2001), 87.

CHAPTER TWO—HIGHLIGHTS AND WISDOM

- The question of who has authority over us and how we relate to them is a key determinant in our ability to walk in victory in these times. Our ability to relate to others will influence the level of success we will be able to attain.

- It is important to remember that submission is, first of all, an attitude. Submission is primarily revealed in the attitude of our hearts toward those God has placed over us.

- Our ability to embrace the principle of submission may make the difference in whether we will be able to fulfill our destiny in God or not.

- There is a way we ought to conduct ourselves in submission to authority and in humility, which is in resonance with the season of life we are in.

- To submit to those in authority over us, is to honor God by respecting the authority He has given to those over us.

- True submission is to recognize God's authority on the people occupying positions of authority over us, and to accord heart respect to them because of their God-given authority.

- Many people in our study did not choose the authority placed over them. Likewise, we should let God lead and guide us in His selection of who will be the spiritual authority in our lives.

- God speaks to us through the leaders He has set in authority over us. If we choose to despise and disregard them, we will never hear the voice of God through them.

- Submission is a powerful tool that God uses to put us in a position where He can get us ready for His calling and purposes.

- To obey a calling means to be willing to go through tutelage and submit ourselves, just like Jesus (who is our pattern) did, so that our gifts and calling can be developed in a safe environment of submission. God will always give the authorities over your life enough information to make the right move for the phase of your life you need to enter.

CHAPTER THREE

The Knowledge of God Equips Us

Accessing the knowledge of God is a key to victory in these days.

Daniel represents a picture of what you and I—indeed, the Church—ought to look and function like in these last days. In these days, we shall witness problems and challenges on earth that human wisdom will have no answer for. The wisdom of the wise shall fail.

THE KNOWLEDGE OF GOD PROVIDES ANSWERS TO UNSOLVABLE PROBLEMS

Many countries and nations now face challenges that seem unsolvable. And in truth, these problems will remain unresolved in the natural world. For example, my country by birth, Nigeria, seems to have such problems. We are greatly blessed with human and natural resources. We have good land for agriculture, a great climate, abundant mineral resources, and highly skilled human resources; yet the poverty level is one of the highest in the world. Corruption, mismanagement, and so many other factors have bedeviled the nation and its economy. We have many churches, yet it seems as though the lives of the people are not changing. There really seems to be no solutions to these problems.

These difficulties persist because the enemy knows these are the last days. He is raising people in the secular world—kings like Nebuchadnezzar—to subdue and rule over the world. It is in these times that those who are like Daniel and his friends must arise. It is this "Daniel company" who will subject the systems of this world to the God they serve. They will arise with answers to seemingly unsolvable problems that face nations.

It is not enough to attend church. Being born-again and speaking in tongues is just the beginning. There must be an intimate fellowship with the Holy Ghost. We must walk in such intimacy that the Holy Spirit will be able to reveal God's mind to us at any given time.

It seems as though God sometimes hides victory and promotion for His children behind unsolvable problems. However, the very problems the world has no answers for are the problems designed to bring the children of God into their destinies. The *real problem* has never been the problem or the challenge. The real problem has been a lack of intimacy with the Holy Ghost.

Jesus stated clearly that the Holy Spirit will show us things to come, and He will reveal the things of God to us (see John 14:26). When we have an intimate fellowship with the Holy Ghost, He will reveal the mind of God to us. He opens us up to the knowledge of God. It takes the knowledge of God to be strong and *to do*.

THE KNOWLEDGE OF GOD CAN HELP US TO INTERPRET DREAMS

Chapter 2 of the Book of Daniel opens with the king having a dream. This dream was given to the king by God.

And in the second year of the reign of Nebuchadnezzar, Nebuchadnezzar dreamed dreams, wherewith his spirit was troubled, and his sleep brake from him. Then the king commanded to call the magicians, and the astrologers, and the sorcerers, and the Chaldeans, for to shew the king his dreams. So they came and stood before the king. And the king said unto them, I have dreamed a dream, and my spirit was troubled to know the dream. Then spake the Chaldeans to the king in Syriack, O king, live for ever: tell thy servants the dream, and we will shew the interpretation. The king answered and said to the Chaldeans, The thing is gone from me: if ye will not make known unto me the dream, with the interpretation thereof, ye shall be cut in pieces, and your houses shall be made a dunghill. But if ye shew the dream, and the interpretation thereof, ye shall receive of me gifts and rewards and great honour: therefore shew me the dream, and the interpretation thereof. They answered again and said, Let the king tell his servants the dream, and we will shew the interpretation of it. The king answered and said, I know of certainty that ye would gain the time, because ye see the thing is gone from me. But if ye will not make known unto me the dream, there is but one decree for you: for ye have prepared lying and corrupt words to speak before me, till the time be changed: therefore tell me the dream, and I shall know that ye can shew me the interpretation thereof (Daniel 2:1-9).

God caused the king to remember that he had a dream, but to forget what the dream was. A real problem? Sure it was! This was a problem that troubled the whole nation. The lives of the magicians, astrologers, Daniel, and his companions were at stake. The magicians and astrologers acknowledged that what the king asked was impossible for man to do. There was no natural solution to the challenge. Thank God for Daniel and his friends.

Daniel had a relationship with God. He knew God! The knowledge of God is the key to victory in these days. Many people place emphasis on what they know; yet what we know will fail. The solution came to Daniel not because of *what* he knew but because of *Who* he knew. Who we know will determine our victory behind enemy lines. Daniel did not consult the books of the magicians or read the books of the astrologers; he consulted the God of Heaven. Who do *you* know?

Listen to me, Church! Many people are trying to figure out their problems by themselves. It is causing heart failure among many. All the thinking, scheming, and planning will not help. We will be able to overcome challenges in our lives and in the nations around us only when we learn the secret of contacting the God of Heaven.

The king had a dream but could not remember the dream. How can a dream be interpreted when even the person who dreamt it cannot remember it? That is what I call an impossible situation. When problems without a solution surface, I pray that the Daniel company will be in position. The day of promotion will not come the way most of us think it will; it will come disguised as an answer to a problem that no one else can solve.

It is only those who can interpret the dreams that God gives, who can provide answers to the mysteries, who will enter into the victories that God has ordained for them. Pharaoh was another king who had a dream that no one could interpret. But there was a man in the kingdom in whom the Spirit of God dwelt; his name was Joseph.

The day of promotion will not come
the way most of us think it will; it will
come disguised as an answer to a
problem that no one else can solve.

Joseph walked with God; he knew God. The Bible calls Joseph a prosperous man because God was with him. Because Joseph knew God and had intimacy with Him, he was able to access the knowledge of God. Let's look at what Joseph did when Pharaoh asked for his help:

> *Pharaoh said to Joseph, "I had a dream, and no one can inter-*
> *pret it. But I have heard it said of you that when you hear a*
> *dream you can interpret it." "I cannot do it," Joseph replied to*
> *Pharaoh, "but God will give Pharaoh the answer he desires"*
> (Genesis 41:15–16 NIV).

Joseph explained that God would give Pharaoh the answer he desired. Joseph acknowledged that it was God who would enable him to interpret Pharaoh's dream.

THE KNOWLEDGE OF GOD GIVES US STRENGTH AND WISDOM

Many people have problems they cannot solve because they focus on *what* they know, not on *Who* they know. I am not writing about knowing man, but knowing God. What we know will come to an end; what we know will fail; what we know cannot stand the test of time; what we know cannot handle the challenges of tomorrow. It is our knowledge of Him that will lead us into a victorious tomorrow. When we know Him, He will show us the way.

Let's look at the story of David, Goliath, and Saul. In First Samuel chapter 17, we see that the Philistines had gathered their forces for war, and that Saul and the Israelites had drawn up a battle line to meet them. The Philistines had a champion named Goliath; he was huge and incredibly strong. Goliath taunted the ranks of Israel: "Choose a man and have him come down to me. If he is able to fight and kill me, we will become your subjects; but if I overcome him and kill him, you will become our subjects and serve us" (1 Sam. 8-9 NIV).

Goliath had challenged Saul and his soldiers; everyone (on both sides) thought that Goliath was too tall and too big to be defeated. All the training the Israelites had undergone in military school had not prepared them for someone of Goliath's size. They were faced with a situation bigger than their knowledge could handle.

But then there was David. David had no military training, no knowledge of warfare tactics or strategy. He had never been in the army nor commanded men. All he had been in charge of during his life was a few sheep. But he knew God! In these days what you know may fail you, but Who you know will sustain you. It was not what David knew, but Who he knew.

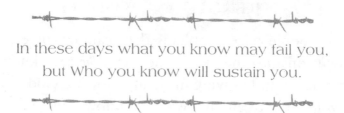

In these days what you know may fail you,
but Who you know will sustain you.

David had cultivated a relationship with God in the quiet of the wilderness. He had enjoyed close communion and fellowship with the Most High. He had known and experienced the love and faithfulness of God. To him, the knowledge of God was not simply information about God contained in the law of Moses; it was a personal, intimate relationship. God knew David, too. God knew where he was and could go to him whenever He wanted.

David had the knowledge of God. This was why, even when facing a giant like Goliath, David knew that before the God whom he served, Goliath was no better than an animal, an uncircumcised Philistine (see 1 Sam. 17:36). This was the knowledge that propelled David to act; it caused him to run toward a giant that every trained soldier had been running from. He ran toward Goliath in the name of the Lord, and the victory was given to him (see 1 Sam. 17:48-49). One man with the knowledge of God was able to defeat what had caused a king and an army of trained soldiers to be terrified, dismayed, and running away in great fear of (see 1 Sam. 17:11,24 NIV).

What are the Goliaths challenging the Church today? What are the Goliaths in your own life? Have you been coming against Goliath based on *what* you know or based on *Who* you know? God will allow Goliaths to arise. Why? Because He wants the Daniels and Davids to walk in victory. Daniels, Davids, and Josephs are those who have cultivated a lifestyle of intimacy, a deep walk with God that has produced knowledge of Him who knows all things.

God will allow Goliaths to arise. Why?
Because He wants the Daniels and
Davids to walk in victory.

In this chapter we have looked at what the knowledge of God can enable us to do. It can provide us answers to unsolvable problems; it can give us strength and wisdom; it can even help us to interpret dreams. But what *is* the knowledge of God? What does it encompass? This will be the topic of our next chapter.

CHAPTER THREE—HIGHLIGHTS AND WISDOM

- In these days we shall witness problems and challenges on earth that human wisdom will have no answer for. Those who are like Daniel and his friends will arise with the answers to the seemingly unsolvable problems facing the nations.

- The very problems the world has no answers for are the problems designed to bring the children of God into their destinies. The *real problem* has never been the problem or the challenge. The real problem has been a lack of intimacy with the Holy Ghost.

- When we have an intimate fellowship with the Holy Ghost, He will reveal the mind of God to us. He opens us up to the knowledge of God. It takes the knowledge of God to be strong and *to do*.

- The solution came to Daniel not because of *what* he knew but because of *Who* he knew. Who we know will determine our victory behind enemy lines.

- We will be able to overcome challenges in our lives and in the nations only when we learn the secret of contacting the God of Heaven.

CHAPTER FOUR

Aspects of the Knowledge of God

Understanding the knowledge of God is a key to victory in these days.

In the previous chapter, we looked at what the knowledge of God can equip us to do. Now let's consider what is contained in the knowledge of God. First we will take a closer look at some aspects or dimensions of the knowledge of God. We will consider four facets: who God is, what He can do, what He wants to do, and our role in what He wants to do. Then we will discuss the importance of having a renewed mind in order to receive the knowledge of God.

THE KNOWLEDGE OF WHO GOD IS

Reverential fear of God is the key that opens the door leading to the knowledge of who God is. God reveals Himself to those who fear Him (see Ps. 25:9-14; Prov. 1:7,29; 2:1-5). In this dimension of the knowledge of God, only God can reveal Himself to us. He must be self-revealing. We have no way of accessing this knowledge without His help. An attitude of reverence and fear is the prerequisite for us to receive the revelation of God. God is all-knowing, so knowing Him also opens us to knowing something of His knowledge. Whenever God gives us an opportunity to know some of what He knows, we have come into favor with Him, and a response of faith and obedience is the least we should do.

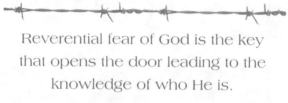

Reverential fear of God is the key
that opens the door leading to the
knowledge of who He is.

It is important to remember that the knowledge of who God is precedes knowing what He knows. God wants us to know Him more than anything else. It is knowing Him that produces strength to do things. As it says in Daniel: "And such as do wickedly against the covenant shall he corrupt by flatteries: but the people that do know their God shall be strong, and do exploits" (Dan. 11:32). And in Philippians, it says, "That I may know Him, and the power of His resurrection, and the fellowship of His sufferings, being made conformable unto His death" (Phil. 3:10).

Truly, knowing Him will lead us to knowing what He knows. In the place of intimacy, He will share His knowledge with His friends. For instance, the Bible records that "Noah walked with God" (Gen. 6:9). *Walk* in this context suggests intimacy. In essence, Noah was intimate with God. He knew

Him! As a result of his knowledge of who God is, God could share the knowledge of what He knew with him.

The story of the flood is a good example of this. When God told Noah about the flood, He revealed some knowledge of His plans to Noah. Every Word from God is self-revelatory. He shares His knowledge, and we have the privilege of knowing Him through knowing what He knows. Every instruction from God is an open door to an experience with God. We need to prepare our hearts to know Him, obey Him in love, and honor Him with all that we have.

THE KNOWLEDGE OF WHAT GOD CAN DO

We know what God can do because we can see what He has done. Many events are recorded in the Bible for us. Our response to this should be praise. "I will bless the Lord at all times: His praise shall continually be in my mouth" (Ps. 34:1).

We were created to praise. We tend to look for what to praise in many areas of our lives. Sometimes we praise cars, celebrities, products, and so many different things. Yet He who deserves our praise is often left out completely. The Book of Psalms says that His praise should continually be on our lips, that He inhabits the praises of His people (see Ps. 34:1; 22:3).

When Paul and Silas prayed and praised God, He showed up in the prison to deliver them (see Acts 16:25-26). When we praise Him, we may experience a demonstration of what He can do. Praising God can silence the enemy if we do it continually in faith.

Look at what He has done. Base your praise on that, and in faith, count on His ability to do much more. Approach His presence with praise and an attitude of expectation for what He can do. Listen to what He has to say and keep your attitude of praise intact. Magnify Him in your heart.

The secret of David's victory over Goliath, among other things, was that he had magnified God in his heart beyond Goliath's size or words. His God was bigger than his fear of Goliath. Praise is the key to magnifying God in your life. Are your problems bigger than God? Spend time praising God, and in your heart He will grow bigger than your problems. What you think about and talk about grows bigger inside of you. Praise God at all times.

The secret of David's victory over Goliath, among other things, was that he had magnified God in his heart beyond Goliath's size or words.

THE KNOWLEDGE OF WHAT GOD WANTS TO DO

The knowledge of what God wants to do can be examined in three parts:

- What He will do.
- What He will allow to happen.
- What He will not allow to happen.

God often chooses to do things in response to our prayers and faith in Him. Mark chapter 5 tells of Jairus, one of the rulers of the synagogue, going to see Jesus. Jairus' daughter was sick, and "Seeing Jesus, he fell at His feet and pleaded earnestly with Him, 'My little daughter is dying. Please come and put Your hands on her so that she will be healed and live'" (Mark 5:22-23 NIV). That is prayer in its simplest form.

Jesus responded to Jairus' plea and went with him. Before they could reach Jairus' home, however, news came that the daughter had died, but Jesus told Jairus, "Don't be afraid; just believe" (Mark 5:36 NIV). I believe Jesus was trying to teach Jairus that his prayers had already set in motion the healing of his daughter, and a negative report should not negate the faith of this man in Jesus. Fear will try to steal your faith; do not let it happen.

In this same chapter of Mark, another miracle is described, but in this case the person in need did not ask Jesus for help (see Mark 5:24-34). The woman with the issue of blood forced her way through the crowd, touched the hem of Jesus' garment, and she was healed of her ailment.

> At once Jesus realized that power had gone out from Him. He turned around in the crowd and asked, "Who touched My clothes?"... Then the woman, knowing what had happened to her, came and fell at His feet and, trembling with fear, told Him the whole truth. He said to her, "Daughter, your faith has healed you. Go in peace and be freed from your suffering" (Mark 5:30,33-34 NIV).

God wants to do things in response to our prayers and faith. If we get on our knees and pray, according to His Word, and believe (and fear not), we will receive answers to our prayers.

God will also allow things to happen when certain conditions are met. In Romans chapter 1, we read how God gave people up to uncleanness; He gave them up to vile affections; He gave them over to a reprobate mind (see Rom. 1:24-28). He allowed this because of what they chose to do with the knowledge of

God that they had. When we make certain choices, God allows the repercussions in our lives.

Many question why God allows things to happen in our lives. If we stay in His presence long enough, and He chooses to let us know, then He will reveal to us why things happen the way they do. For example, when sin goes unconfessed, satan is given legal ground to devastate our lives.

When we stand in faith and have vital contact with God, God will not allow the forces of evil to prevail over us. Many times, however, we ignore the battle until it is too late to fight back effectively. Many live lives of ease and put on the whole armor of God only when the battle is at their doorstep.

God has ordained laws in all realms of life. We cannot disregard these laws and expect God to keep holding back the repercussions from our lives. For example, the Bible says, "death and life are in the power of the tongue" (Prov. 18:21). We may use our mouths to sow seeds of death, and then when the harvest comes, we ask why God allowed it. He put the law into motion. He did not allow the harvest; we caused the law to work against us.

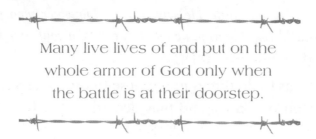

Many live lives of and put on the
whole armor of God only when
the battle is at their doorstep.

THE KNOWLEDGE OF OUR ROLE IN WHAT HE WANTS TO DO

When God wants to do something on the earth, He usually works through people. He desires that we play a part in His plan. Some men want to play no part and simply want to see things happen to them. But by His Spirit, God inspires us into action, which will lead to the miracles we need. Whenever we are praying for God to do things in our life, we should ask to know what our role is in what He wants to do in response to our faith.

I wonder who told blind Bartimaeus to shout louder to get Jesus' attention? Who informed the woman with the issue of blood that she could draw on the power of God through the hem of Jesus' garment? We must remember that walking with God will always require faith, but He also desires to reveal Himself by working with us.

We should not let any strongholds keep us from walking in the knowledge of God. The way to identify existing strongholds is to recognize the reactions that pop up in our minds whenever the knowledge of God comes to us. Usually, what God tells us to do may look ridiculous, but sometimes the ridiculous precedes the miraculous. Our future lies in our knowledge of God. We are to seek after all that God has for us! Amen!

THE KNOWLEDGE OF GOD REQUIRES A RENEWED MIND

The key to lasting victory in our lives is our knowledge of God. The knowledge of God includes knowing His ways, His plans, His purposes, and His timing. We will also need to know how God's Kingdom functions and the implications of our humanity. To know the will of God we need to have our minds renewed. As it says in Romans chapter 12:

I beseech you therefore, brethren, by the mercies of God, that ye present your bodies a living sacrifice, holy, acceptable unto

*God, which is your reasonable service. And be not conformed
to this world: but be ye transformed by the renewing of your
mind, that ye may prove what is that good, and acceptable, and
perfect, will of God* (Romans 12:1-2).

In these verses, presenting the body precedes renewing the
mind. A body not presented to God will not have a renewable
mind. However, the process will start with the mind embracing offering the body. The mind must first embrace offering
the body as a living sacrifice before renewal can begin. The
mind and the body influence one another. We also need to remember that Paul is addressing Christians in these verses. Paul
is addressing a process that will lead Christians into victory. It
starts with presenting the body.

The mind is renewed when its internal configuration is
brought into harmony with the available knowledge of God.
Because the knowledge of God is progressive, renewing the
mind must also be an ongoing process in the life of the believer.
We will never get to the place where we can say we fully know
God. God keeps revealing different dimensions of Himself to us.
As He imparts a dimension of Himself to us, we must allow the
knowledge of that dimension to cause an internal reconfigura-
tion of our minds. Our minds, expectations, and perceptions
must be brought into harmony with the new knowledge that is
revealed to us. Our expectations and outlook must be based on
the knowledge revealed. This is the process of mind renewal.
This is also the reason why it never ends. As we grow in our
walk with Him, He unveils more and more of Himself, and we
keep renewing our mind in the light of that unveiling.

Our minds have been affected by the sin inherited from
Adam; they have been programmed for selfishness, pride (as a
cover for insecurity and low self-esteem), and fear, among

other shortcomings. This programming can be negatively compounded by the type of our personal upbringing we have, coupled with our cultural environment, and other peculiar experiences had in life.

As we grow in our walk with Him,
He unveils more and more of Himself, and we keep renewing our
mind in the light of that unveiling.

Renewal of our minds is designed to change us from the inside out. The Kingdom of God is first and foremost an internal affair. God usually works on the inside to produce a change that will affect both the internal state and the external experiences of man. To *conform* implies "being molded externally" or "being squeezed into an external mold." To be *transformed* implies "allowing an internal mold to determine the direction of our lives." The Kingdom of God is an internal affair first and foremost.

We still have a choice like Adam had. We can either choose to eat from the tree of the knowledge of good and evil or to eat from the tree of life. Since the fall of man, I believe *choosing to eat from the tree of the knowledge of good and evil* means "the choice or decision for good or evil arrived at independently of God." It is the good that sets the trap for us to fall into the evil. Whenever we choose good or evil without the aid of God's Spirit, we run the risk of eating from that tree again and again. Our choices must be influenced by the Spirit and the Word of God. It is only then that we can truly say that we live by the tree of life (Christ) and not by leaning on our own understanding. As it says in

Proverbs, you are to "Trust in the Lord with all your heart and lean not on your own understanding" (Prov. 3:5 NIV).

Many people attempt to change certain behavior patterns but find it difficult to sustain the change if their minds are not renewed. Until what is inside the mind is changed (by renewal), the changes in behavior will not be permanent. The body can be controlled by the mind. What the mind does not permit, the body usually cannot do. To break a habit, we must first break the thought pattern that governs the habit. It is only after breaking the mind (the thought pattern) that the mind and the spirit can join forces to cause a permanent change in the negative behavioral patterns manifested through the body. Our minds can then be free to receive signals from the Spirit of God when the renewal process is underway. Paul told Timothy to study to show himself approved unto God (see 2 Tim. 2:15 KJV). The word "study" (*spoudazo* in Greek) and in other translations implies "to give diligence, make effort, thinking and acting, planning and producing" (Strong's Concordance, #4704). You are to make an effort and be consistent as you study God's Word.

To successfully live behind enemy lines we must understand what it means to be consecrated and to live a consecrated life. We also need to understand how we are to relate to those in authority. And as we have learned in the past two chapters, we must understand what the knowledge of God is and how it can be applied in our lives. In the next two chapters, we will discuss another important key to living a successful life: understanding covenants and covenant relationships.

CHAPTER FOUR—HIGHLIGHTS AND WISDOM

- Reverential fear of God is the key that opens the door leading to the knowledge of who God is.

- The key to lasting victories in our lives is our knowledge of God. The knowledge of God includes knowing His ways, His plans, His purposes, and His timing.

- To know the will of God we need to have our minds renewed. The mind is renewed when its internal configuration is brought into harmony with the available knowledge of God.

- The Kingdom of God is first and foremost an internal affair. God usually works on the inside to produce a change that will affect both the internal state and the external experiences of man.

- Since the fall of man, choosing to eat from the tree of the knowledge of good and evil means "the choice or decision for good or evil arrived at independently of God." It is the good that sets the trap for us to fall into the evil.

Covenants and Covenant Relationships

An understanding of covenant relationships—what they are and how they work—is essential if we are to win in these endtimes.

There are no Rambos in the Kingdom! John Rambo was the protagonist in a series of movies that came out of Hollywood a number of years ago. Rambo was a one-man army; he could single-handedly take on an army and defeat it. He would parachute behind enemy lines, take on the enemy, destroy his targets, and come out unscathed. He was a soldier who needed no help, only the right equipment. He could beat the enemy on his own, by himself. This is not so in God's Kingdom.

God has ordained, that for us to win and be successful in Kingdom business, we must work with others. We must have relationships in which there is mutual commitment to one another and toward God and His Kingdom. There are blessings and benefits in covenant relationships, and we should seek to walk in them.

One of the terms used to describe God's people, is the word *body*. The term *body* creates a picture of relationships—parts that are different, yet working together toward a common goal. One individual part does not make a body. It is the parts joined and working together that make a body. The joining of different parts in the body working together is a picture of what covenant relationships are like and are designed to achieve. It is the coming together of people who are committed to God, His Kingdom, and one another, and who are focused on seeing God's Kingdom come and His will done in their lives and on earth.

Covenant relationships are established and ordained by God to fulfill His purpose and establish His Kingdom in the lives of His people and on earth. A compulsory feature of covenant relationships is that they are focused on God and His purposes. Covenant relationships are much more than social or family associations. This does not mean they cannot exist among friends or members of the same family; it simply means the bond that brings people together in a covenant relationship is God—not family or friendship.

People in covenant relationships are bound together by a pact. This pact is beyond convenience; it is based on commitment. To understand covenant relationships we must understand covenant. Many people use the term *covenant* without knowing what covenant is or what it involves.

Our God is a covenant-keeping God. The Bible is an account of God's covenant dealings with man. God is the originator of covenant, and therefore there can be no true understanding of covenant outside of Him. The enemy always attempts to pervert the things that God does. What we see and understand as covenant today, may not necessarily be even close to what God meant covenant or covenant relationships to be.

A compulsory feature of covenant
relationships is that they are focused
on God and His purposes.

WHAT IS COVENANT?

Covenant is defined as "a mutual understanding, an agreement, a solemn undertaking, a contract that is legally binding, or a signed agreement in writing between two or more parties, with respect to a promise or a commitment." In the Bible, covenant involves promise, commitment, faithfulness, and loyalty even to death. It was considered so sacred that the parties involved did not enter into it lightly; a person was as good as his covenant word.

In the Body of Christ, true believers are in a covenant relationship with God through Christ. We are also in covenant relationship with each other. This, for example, is symbolized each time we gather around the Lord's table for the covenant meal (Holy Communion), during which we partake of His broken body and His shed blood.

From the beginning of creation, God's power and might have been and are still being manifested or perpetuated through His covenants. God governs the universe and this entire creation by covenant ordinances. An example of the power of God being perpetuated in His covenants can be seen in the Book of Jeremiah:

Thus saith the Lord; If ye can break My covenant of the day, and My covenant of the night, and that there should not be day and night in their season; Then may also My covenant be broken with David My servant, that he should not have a son to reign upon his throne; and with the Levites the priests, My ministers. As the host of heaven cannot be numbered, neither the sand of the sea measured: so will I multiply the seed of David My servant, and the Levites that minister unto Me. Moreover the word of the Lord came to Jeremiah, saying, Considerest thou not what this people have spoken, saying, The two families which the Lord hath chosen, He hath even cast them off? Thus they have despised My people, that they should be no more a nation before them. Thus saith the Lord; If My covenant be not with day and night, and if I have not appointed the ordinances of heaven and earth; Then will I cast away the seed of Jacob and David My servant, so that I will not take any of his seed to be rulers over the seed of Abraham, Isaac, and Jacob: for I will cause their captivity to return, and have mercy on them (Jeremiah 33:20-26).

Another example of God's power being manifested in His covenants can be found in Genesis chapter 8:

And the Lord smelled a sweet savour; and the Lord said in His heart, I will not again curse the ground any more for man's sake; for the imagination of man's heart is evil from his youth; neither will I again smite any more every thing living, as I have done. While the earth remaineth, seedtime and harvest, and cold and heat, and summer and winter, and day and night shall not cease (Genesis 8:21-22).

In fact, God upholds all things including our lives by "the word of His power" (Heb.1:3). Every word that proceeds out of God's mouth is His covenant bond. What He says becomes a covenant word that cannot be broken (see Ps. 89:34).

Many people today have no clue what a covenant looks like or what it means. Their predominant thoughts about what a covenant is or is not are often contrary to God's thoughts.

In contrast, the spirit underlying a covenant mind-set can be seen in a traditional, biblical Jewish family. In such a family, the father took his place, with all his strength and might, and was given the freedom to be the father. The mother took her place and the children theirs. In such a family—where the spirit of covenant was at work—there was loyalty, faithfulness, consistency, and commitment to one another and to the family. This was learned from the God of Abraham.

If we are to be victorious Christians, we must understand that God is a covenant-minded God. Too many of us struggle in our walk with God because our thoughts are so far removed from this reality. God thinks covenant, we think convenience; God thinks covenant, we think comfort. We do things that are convenient and comfortable for us. God bases His actions on what He has covenanted to do. As I have said earlier, the entire Bible is a covenant book. Every thought of God in the Bible is a covenant thought. Everything that God created and did in Genesis chapter 1 has been kept in place by the power of His covenant. God is a consistent God.

God thinks covenant,
we think convenience;
God thinks covenant,
we think comfort.

COVENANT RELATIONSHIPS BEGIN
WITH KNOWING GOD

For us to understand covenant and walk in covenant relationship, we must first know God. This is the place to start. We cannot begin to think about covenant between ourselves and other human beings without first having a solid understanding of our covenant with God. This is because without a covenant with God, a covenant with human beings can be abused and manipulated.

So, we must start by understanding that God is a covenant God, and He does not recognize any other relationship except covenant relationship. This is why it has been difficult for many believers to walk with God. For many of us, the concept of covenant is far removed from our thinking.

For example, many people wonder in their hearts why God would set apart a people, a nation called Israel, and treat them specially and with so much favor. Such questions arise because we do not understand covenant. God was not looking for a group of people; He had a man in mind (Abraham). It was through this man that a nation came into prominence. It was because of God's covenant with Abraham that the Jews became what they were.

God was not groping in the dark looking for a people. He had a plan, a clear plan. His plan was to take a man, and through covenant with that man, make a way for the Redeemer to redeem the entire human race.

He did not just randomly choose Abraham either. He tested Abraham and made sure He was number one in Abraham's life. He made sure He was the first person in Abraham's life before He entered into covenant with him. Without the covenant that God had with Abraham, the Jewish nation would not even exist. This is why our focus should not be on the Jewish nation; our focus should be on the covenant that gave birth to that nation.

Our understanding of covenant and that God is a covenant God affects more than we realize. Even our ability to interpret and understand the Bible depends on our understanding of covenant and God as a covenant-keeping God. When we read the Bible, it will make less sense to us until we understand His covenant-keeping nature. God needed a covenant with Abraham because that covenant was the strength, permission, and authority for God to do the things that He needed to do in Abraham's life and on earth. Abraham was God's man.

COVENANT INVOLVES SACRIFICE

The first thing that we need to understand about covenant is that it always involves sacrifice. Did Abraham have to sacrifice anything to enter into covenant with God? You better believe it! Before looking at the story of Abraham, let's consider God's own sacrifice.

God gave His only Son as a sacrifice to enter into covenant with us. When we think about this sacrifice, we often focus on the death of Jesus on the cross. But let us really think about His sacrifice—it involved much more! Jesus sacrificed so much. Think about what He went through, how He left glory and lived as a human being. He had to be limited by His humanity; He became a servant, a slave just to identify with us. Then He paid the ultimate price: taking our sins on Himself. Jesus, who had so much intimacy with the Father in His presence, had to endure separation from His Father for our sake; He had to go through death. He endured all that so we could come into covenant with the Father. What awesome sacrifice!

Now let us return to looking at the example of Abraham. When Abraham was called, he was told to leave his father and mother, to leave everything that he could trust and depend on, and to follow the One he could not see. Covenant will always involve sacrifice.

Marriage is an example of a covenant relationship. Many today view marriage as archaic and outdated. And some who are married do not understand the covenant nature of it. One of the reasons why marriages fail is because those involved are not willing to sacrifice anything

But the Bible says, "Wives, submit yourselves unto your own husbands, as unto the Lord," and "Husbands, love your wives, even as Christ also loved the church, and gave Himself for it" (Eph. 5:22,25). According to these verses, marriage involves sacrifice. Questions that arise in the hearts of couples such as, "Why should I love her and lay down my life for her?" or "Why should I submit when I think I am smarter than him?" can be answered only in the light of sacrifice and covenant.

Even in the home, for a covenant to bind
the family together, there must be sacrifice.

Even in the home, for a covenant to bind a family together, there must be sacrifice. Dad and mom must be willing to sacrifice some things for their children. The children must also be willing to sacrifice in obeying their parents, even when they

see their friends doing otherwise. Everybody has to sacrifice or else the covenant in the family will not work.

To walk in covenant relationship, we must understand that sacrifice is involved. We also need to remember that sacrifice started with God Himself. To really understand covenant, all we need to do is to understand God. In the Old Testament, God taught the people of Israel to make sacrifices, not because He was bloodthirsty, but because He wanted the people to understand the value of sacrifice and to prove what was in their hearts. It is not possible to have covenant without sacrifice. This is reflected in the Old Testament meaning of the word *covenant*, which means "the cutting."

I once read a story of two villages somewhere in the jungles of either Africa or South America. One village was made up of farmers. They understood the science of farming and were excellent farmers. The other village was comprised of hunters. They knew little or nothing at all about faming, but they were excellent hunters and warriors. These two villages decided to enter into a covenant with each other. The farmers would farm for the two villages, and the hunters would hunt for and protect both villages.

On the day designated for formalizing the agreement, there was a big gathering and celebration. The people from both villages had a feast. There was plenty of eating and drinking together. Then a representative was chosen from each village, an incision was made on their hands to draw blood, the blood was mixed in drink, and both representatives drank the mixture from the same cup. From that moment, all the people from those villages became blood brothers. They became one! No one could come against one village without the other village rising up to defend it; they became a larger, stronger family.

This story illustrates how the heart of every human being longs for stable, loyal, committed relationships. The only place this can be found is in covenant. We want dependable relationships, and this is what God has come to give us. It is only through Him that we can have such relationships.

In this story, two communities would bring together what they produced through farming and hunting, and then they would distribute it fairly. They were a bigger family; it was a better life and future for both villages. This is what God had in mind when He ordained covenant relationships. He had a plan that would give those in covenant a bigger and better life and future.

Unfortunately, we find that there are things that work against God's covenant and God's plan. I am talking about our human flesh and human desires. These can work against God's covenant. This is as true for us as it was in the time of Abraham. But even though Abraham had his faults, God still kept His part of the covenant.

When God wanted to enter into covenant with us, He sent His only Son Jesus Christ, and His Son became the sacrificial Lamb. In this covenant, Jesus represented the human race before the Father. When Jesus brought His blood to the Father, the blood was accepted. By that sacrifice and the acceptance of the blood, the family of God and the family of man became united in Jesus Christ. This is why we have the name of Jesus as our own, just like in a marriage covenant. This is why we go in His name.

When we understand covenant and pay the price in sacrifice, we come into a relationship that is better than what we had before, and our future is better guaranteed because of the covenant. But all this can be accessed only when we truly understand sacrifice. When we do, sacrifice no longer becomes a pain, but a function of love; it is no longer a struggle, but a function of understanding the covenant. When we understand that sacrifice is part of what enables the covenant to work, we will embrace it wholeheartedly.

For example, consider a man who worked very hard, became quite rich, died, and left a large inheritance to his children. I am sure you will agree that to sustain and increase what was given to them, the children should embrace the same lifestyle as their father (which resulted in the great wealth he acquired.) If they do not embrace this lifestyle, their inheritance will soon be wasted. We can see this principle at work in the story of the prodigal son.

> *Then He said, "A certain man had two sons. And the younger of them said to his father, 'Father, give me the portion of goods that falls to me.' So he divided to them his livelihood. And not many days after, the younger son gathered all together, journeyed to a far country, and there wasted his possessions with prodigal living. But when he had spent all, there arose a severe famine in that land, and he began to be in want. Then he went and joined himself to a citizen of that country, and he sent him into his fields to feed swine. And he would gladly have filled his stomach with the pods that the swine ate, and no one gave him anything. But when he came to himself, he said, 'How many of my father's hired servants have bread enough and to spare, and I perish with hunger! I will arise and go to my father, and will say to him, Father, I have sinned against heaven, and before you, and I am no longer worthy to be called your son. Make me like one of your hired servants'"* (Luke 15:11-19 NKJV).

The parable illustrates this point. The prodigal son did not embrace the lifestyle of his father, and he soon lost all that he had been given.

Jesus through His sacrifice made it possible for the covenant to be available to us. We can enter, walk in, and enjoy the covenant but only by embracing the life of sacrifice that made it available in the first place. This is how it works. Otherwise we will waste, abuse, and frustrate that grace, which has been made available to us, if we do not embrace the life of sacrifice.

COVENANT INVOLVES RECOGNITION

Another major feature involved in covenant can be seen in Hebrews chapter 2:

> *Inasmuch then as the children have partaken of flesh and blood, He Himself likewise shared in the same; that through death He might destroy him who had the power of death, that is, the devil; and release those who through fear of death were all their lifetime subject to bondage. For indeed He does not give aid to angels; but He does give aid to the seed of Abraham. Therefore in all things He had to be made like His brethren, that He might be a merciful and faithful High Priest in things pertaining to God, to make propitiation for the sins of the people. For in that He Himself has suffered, being tempted, He is able to aid those who are tempted* (Hebrews 2:14-18 NKJV).

In covenant, there must be recognition of the true state of the parties involved. Jesus recognized our true state. One of the greatest challenges that we face as human beings is to recognize and acknowledge our true state. We all have our own little worlds, created by our mind-sets. We all think we are good. This brings conflict.

If we do not see ourselves the way God (our Covenant Partner) sees us, we cannot enter into a true covenant relationship. We must acknowledge God's reality. Until we see ourselves the way God sees us, we will not truly accept the sacrifice that He made to restore us to the way we ought to be: His covenant partners. This is why in covenant it is absolutely necessary for the parties to recognize their true state.

For example, when the parties involved in a marriage covenant fail to recognize their true state, they will not submit to the grace that God has placed in their spouse to help them. When a husband recognizes that he is not graced in business and financial matters, he should be willing to submit to his covenant partner, his wife, if she is graced in such areas. In the same way, if the wife is not graced in relationships and handling people and the husband is, the wife should be willing and ready to submit to her husband who is graced in such an area. But this will not happen until both parties come to terms with their true state, that is, the grace peculiar to them.

When the parties involved in a marriage covenant fail to recognize their true state, they will not submit to the grace that God has placed in their spouse to help them.

As long as the husband has a mind-set of, "I am the head of this home; I decide what financial and business decisions are made," and his wife thinks, "I am the woman; I ought to determine relationship issues," there can be no true enjoyment of covenant. This is because there has been a failure to recognize their true state.

In the earlier example of the two villages, what made the covenant strong was the fact that both parties recognized their true state. The farmers recognized that their own strength was farming. They did not try to take the place of the hunters. The hunters recognized that their weakness was farming, so they submitted to the strength of the farmers in that area. This is what it takes for covenant relationships to work.

With regard to God, He has no weaknesses, so we are to submit to God in all things to walk in covenant with Him. Often, we think we are smarter than God! We may never say so, but our actions indicate this mind-set. This is why we take matters into our own hands. We disobey God's Word, we do what we consider best (and we actually expect to prosper), and we run our lives our own way.

In covenant we must recognize our true state. We must come to terms with the fact that we are nothing, have nothing, can do nothing, and know nothing compared to God. It is only in covenant with Him, in submitting to God and His Word, that we become what we are in Christ Jesus. As long as we recognize our true state, we will always fall on the mercy and wisdom of God. This is what covenant demands.

COVENANT INVOLVES DEFINED ROLES

From the passage in Hebrews mentioned earlier, we can identify another feature of covenants: Covenants involve defined roles (see Heb. 2:14-18). Roles must be defined in a covenant. It is not enough for the parties to recognize their true state; they must also identify the roles that they have been called to fulfill.

God's role, where we are concerned is Redeemer, Savior, Lord, and Master. What is our role? We are beneficiaries of the sacrifice of Jesus Christ. We are honored to be called of God. We have His life in us, and as we have received His life, we are to respond to His purposes. We should not play God over our life nor anyone else's life. We are recipients of His grace, and when things get tough in our lives and we cannot save ourselves, we know who to run to—His name is Jesus!

Recognizing roles solves many problems. Some people want to play God over their lives and the lives of others. No one has given us this role! We are God's children once we are saved and in covenant with Him. God has His standards, and He wants to give us His grace so that we can measure up to His standards. But every time we fall short, we have a Savior! We never outgrow the need for a Savior and Redeemer. If we could fix our own lives and solve our own problems, we would not need a savior. This is what recognizing roles is all about.

It is clear that recognizing roles will be possible only when we admit our true state. A person who is living in a dream world as far as his true state is concerned, will assume a role not designed for him in the covenant. An example of this can be seen in First Samuel chapter 13:

> *And some of the Hebrews crossed over the Jordan to the land of Gad and Gilead. As for Saul, he was still in Gilgal, and all the people followed him trembling. Then he waited seven days, according to the time set by Samuel. But Samuel did not come to Gilgal; and the people were scattered from him. So Saul said, "Bring a burnt offering and peace offerings here to me." And he offered the burnt offering. Now it happened, as soon as he finished presenting the burnt offering, that Samuel came; and Saul went out to meet him, that he might greet him. And*

Samuel said, "What have you done?" Saul said, "When I saw that the people were scattered from me, and that you did not come within the days appointed, and that the Philistines gathered together at Michmash, then I said, 'The Philistines will now come down on me at Gilgal, and I have not made supplication to the Lord.' Therefore I felt compelled, and offered a burnt offering." And Samuel said to Saul, "You have done foolishly. You have not kept the commandment of the Lord your God, which He commanded you. For now the Lord would have established your kingdom over Israel forever. But now your kingdom shall not continue. The Lord has sought for Himself a man after His own heart, and the Lord has commanded him to be commander over His people, because you have not kept what the Lord commanded you" (1 Samuel 13:7-14 NKJV).

Saul, who had been anointed king by Samuel, the prophet and priest, assumed a role that was not his. As a result of Saul assuming this role, he lost his kingdom. Remember, that he (and his seed) should have been king over Israel, but because he broke the covenant—by not recognizing his role in the kingdom, among other things—he lost out on the promise of the covenant.

We must remember that recognizing our roles in covenants is a key to determining whether we will continue to enjoy the blessings and benefits of covenant relationships or not.

COVENANT INVOLVES EMBRACING RESPONSIBILITY

What is expected or required of each person in a covenant? Each individual in a covenant will be responsible for something in that relationship. For covenant relationships to work, those involved must know their roles and embrace the responsibility that goes with their role. When someone in a covenant relationship fails to embrace his or her responsibility in the relationship, then he or she becomes a covenant breaker.

For covenant relationships to work,
those involved must know their roles
and embrace the responsibility that
goes with their role.

Let's look at an example of a covenant in Matthew chapter 26:

> *And they were exceedingly sorrowful, and each of them began to say to Him, "Lord, is it I?" He answered and said, "He who dipped his hand with Me in the dish will betray Me. The Son of Man indeed goes just as it is written of Him, but woe to that man by whom the Son of Man is betrayed! It would have been good for that man if he had not been born." Then Judas, who was betraying Him, answered and said, "Rabbi, is it I?" He said to him, "You have said it." And as they were eating, Jesus took bread, blessed and broke it, and gave it to the disciples and said, "Take, eat; this is My body." Then He took the cup, and gave thanks, and gave it to them, saying, "Drink from it, all of you. For this is My blood of the new covenant, which is shed for many for the remission of sins"* (Matthew 26:22-28 NKJV).

The bread and the cup are two items that stand out from the story of when Jesus instituted the Lord's Supper. The bread can be viewed as a symbol of the benefits we enjoy from the covenant we have with God in Jesus. This refers to blessings like healing, prosperity, victory, and so on. When we eat the bread, we acknowledge the benefits or blessings that are ours because of our covenant with God through Christ.

The cup also represents something. Every time Jesus used the word *cup* in relation to Himself, He always spoke of the price He had to pay, the things He was going to suffer to make our covenant with God possible. By drinking the cup, we signify our willingness to embrace our responsibility to pay whatever price will be required of us in the covenant. The cup symbolizes our responsibility in the covenant. It speaks of the responsibility to win souls, the responsibility to walk in love, the responsibility to give, and the responsibility to be willing to lay down our lives if the covenant demands it. It is when we understand our role that embracing our responsibility becomes clear.

COVENANT INVOLVES WORDS OR CONFESSIONS

In Hebrews chapter 3, we see how words or confessions play a role in covenants. "Therefore, holy brethren, partakers of the heavenly calling, consider the Apostle and High Priest of our confession, Christ Jesus" (Heb. 3:1 NKJV).

Words have a very important part to play in any covenant relationship. When a covenant is made, words are spoken. For instance, in the example of the two villages that we have been examining, words something like this were probably said, "From this day forward, these two tribes have become one. Let this becoming one, be binding on each part—on every family member and every member of these tribes."

These kinds of words or declarations carry tremendous weight. In the New Testament, we also have declarations; they are the doctrines or creeds of the apostles. The apostles would come together and make certain declarations: "We believe in Jesus; we believe He is the Son of God; we believe He died and rose from the dead; we believe He is coming to take us home." These declarations are necessary for the working of the covenant.

At a wedding, confessions (the words spoken) bring two people into the covenant of marriage. The bride and groom stand before a servant of God and before witnesses. They confess their willingness to take one another as husband and wife. They bind themselves until "death do us part." It is their confession that initiates the covenant relationship. It is also our confession that initiates our covenant with God through Jesus Christ. We confess with our mouth the Lord Jesus and are saved (see Rom. 10:9-10).

Covenant relationships are initiated by confessions, declarations, or words spoken. What some of us have failed to realize, is that the covenant will also be sustained and strengthened by our words. The confessions of the husband and wife will build their home and increase the love they have for one another. The more the parties confess their love for one another, the more that love will be built up and strengthened. The same is also true about our covenant with God. The more we confess and declare what the Word says about who we are in Christ and our love for God, the more we are built up and strengthened.

"I am the righteousness of God in Christ Jesus! Greater is He that is in me, than he that is in the world! I am a royal priesthood, a holy nation, a peculiar people, called out of darkness to radiate the glory of God" (see 2 Cor. 5:21; 1 John 4:4; 1 Pet. 2:9). These are not mere empty words! They are confessions of our faith, and the Bible clearly states that Jesus is the High Priest of our confession (see Heb. 3:1 NKJV).

Jesus takes these words into Heaven, stands before the Father as our High Priest, and presents these words to Him. In essence, we activate the blessings of the covenant by saying or declaring what the covenant says about the dimension we want to activate. Jesus takes those covenant words to the Father, the Father honors the covenant words, grace is released, and we are strengthened in that dimension of the covenant.

Covenant is built on words, established with words, and released by words! We must be very conscious of our covenant with God and our covenants with one another. This covenant consciousness changes our perspective, and the change in our perspective changes our words. This is another reason why our confessions are very important in covenants. The more we confess the Word of God, the greater our consciousness of our covenant with Him becomes.

One of the reasons God changed Abram's name to Abraham, was to strengthen his consciousness of the covenant. *Abraham* means "father of nations." Every time Abraham heard his new name, he was reminded of God's promise, and his consciousness of the covenant was strengthened. Abraham's name became a daily confession that strengthened him in his covenant with God.

Like Abraham, we must also confess or declare daily those words that remind us of God's promises. Doing so will strengthen our consciousness of His covenant with us. It is the strength of this consciousness that produces our ability to demonstrate covenant life and power.

Now that we have some understanding of what covenants and covenant relationships are, it's time to look more closely at the purpose of covenant relationships. This will be our topic in the next chapter.

CHAPTER FIVE—HIGHLIGHTS AND WISDOM

- God has ordained, that for us to win and be successful in Kingdom business, we must work with others. In the Body of Christ, true believers are in a covenant relationship with God through Christ. We are also in covenant relationship with each other.

- To walk in covenant relationship, we must understand that sacrifice is involved. We also need to remember that sacrifice started with God Himself. It is not possible to have covenant without sacrifice.

- Human flesh and desires work against the covenant.

- When we understand covenant and pay the price in sacrifice, we come into a relationship that is better than what we had before, and our future is better guaranteed because of the covenant.

- In covenant we must recognize our true state. We must come to terms with the fact that we are nothing, have nothing, can do nothing, and know nothing compared to God.

- It is not enough for the parties to recognize their true state; they must also identify the roles that they have been called to fulfill.

- Covenant relationships are initiated by confessions, declarations, or words spoken.

The Purpose of Covenant Relationships

An understanding of the purpose of covenant relationships is essential if we are to win in these endtimes.

It is not enough to have a covenant relationship with God alone. Although this—as I have emphasized—must be the starting point, we must also understand that God expects us to have our "own company": people with whom we are in covenant relationship. There are several Scriptures that illustrate this point.

In Ecclesiastes it says, "Two are better than one; because they have a good reward for their labour" (Eccles. 4:9). And in Genesis, it says, "And the Lord God said, 'It is not good that man should be alone; I will make him a helper comparable to him" (Gen. 2:18 NKJV). These two Scriptures establish that God expects us to have relationships with other people, relationships that are focused on Him. It is as we walk in covenant relationship with others that we will be able to maximize the potential of God in us.

COVENANT RELATIONSHIPS ENCOURAGE US

Covenant relationships are designed to lift us up; they are designed to strengthen and encourage us. Our Lord Jesus gave us an example of how covenant relationships ought to operate. His example is described in Matthew chapter 26:

> *Then cometh Jesus with them unto a place called Gethsemane, and saith unto the disciples, Sit ye here, while I go and pray yonder. And He took with Him Peter and the two sons of Zebedee, and began to be sorrowful and very heavy. Then saith He unto them, My soul is exceeding sorrowful, even unto death: tarry ye here, and watch with me* (Matthew 26:36–38).

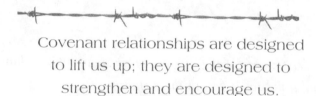

Covenant relationships are designed
to lift us up; they are designed to
strengthen and encourage us.

This was a critical time in the life and ministry of Jesus. He was about to go to the cross and face separation from the Father. It was not an event He looked forward to. However, this was the very reason He came to earth. Jesus needed strength to face the assignment ahead, and He decided to pray. The outstanding thing is that, even though He was the Son of God and had the Spirit of God without measure, He chose to have His disciples with Him at this hour. He did not go it alone!

In fact, Jesus actually asked for help! Notice though that He did not ask the multitudes to help Him, neither did He call on all His disciples. He chose those with whom He had established a close covenant relationship, and He asked for their help in His time of need. Remember that earlier He had said they were no longer servants but friends.

> *Henceforth I call you not servants; for the servant knoweth not what his lord doeth: but I have called you friends; for all things that I have heard of My Father I have made known unto you* (John 15:15).

Friend is a covenant word; it is used to describe more than an ordinary, casual relationship. It speaks of a relationship based on covenant. The Lord and Master, in His time of need, decided to call on those with whom He had a covenant relationship to help Him. By this, He set an example, showing that we need covenant relationships to walk victoriously in life.

We must also remember that these disciples who were called by Jesus had been tested in their commitment to Him.

> *From that time many of His disciples went back and walked with Him no more. Then Jesus said to the twelve, "Do you also want to go away?" But Simon Peter answered Him, "Lord, to whom shall we go? You have the words of eternal life. Also we have come to believe and know that You are the Christ, the Son of the living God"* (John 6:66-69 NKJV).

Even though many of the other disciples left Jesus, these stood by His side because they recognized Him for who He truly was. They were committed to Him. Their relationship was beyond convenience; they were committed to Him.

COVENANT RELATIONSHIPS PROTECT AND STRENGTHEN US

All of us will go through challenges; we will face situations that seem insurmountable. One of the weapons we can use to overcome at such times is the covenant relationships that God has established around us. God puts these relationships in place so that we may draw strength from these people even when we are weak. These relationships are usually put in place before the challenge or situation arises.

This principle was at work in the life of Daniel. Daniel was devoted to God, but he also had strong relationships with like-minded friends. In a sense, we can say that he had both horizontal and vertical relationships. In Daniel chapter 2, we read:

> *He answered and said to Arioch the king's captain, "Why is the decree from the king so urgent?" Then Arioch made the decision known to Daniel. So Daniel went in and asked the king to give him time that he might tell the king the interpretation. Then Daniel went to his house, and made the decision known to Hananiah, Mishael, and Azariah, his companions* (Daniel 2:15-17 NKJV).

Daniel went to his companions. God expects us to have our own companions: people with whom we are in covenant relationship and with whom we can stand in agreement to see God's purposes established and His Kingdom advanced.

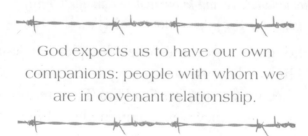

God expects us to have our own companions: people with whom we are in covenant relationship.

This pattern can also be seen in the New Testament. In Acts chapters 3 and 4, Peter and John were arrested for healing a crippled man, and were threatened with punishment if they spoke or taught again in the name of Jesus. "And being let go, they went to their own companions and reported all that the chief priests and elders had said to them. So when they heard that, they raised their voice to God with one accord..." (Acts 4:23-24 NKJV).

It is important to observe that Peter and John had "their own companions." They were not working alone. They had a group of people whom they were in covenant relationship with and with whom they could stand in agreement and lift their voices to God.

God has not designed us to work in isolation. There will be situations where our faith is weak, when we need encouragement and strength to go on. Inasmuch as it is good to encourage ourselves in the Lord, God has already placed people around us with whom He expects us to be in relationship and from whom we can draw encouragement.

Peter and John recognized this, and after they had been threatened, they went to their own companions. God positions our companions around us, so that we can strengthen and encourage one another. There will be times when the enemy's attacks may be too much for us to handle alone. But with the help of one another we will be able to overcome (see Eccles. 4:9-12).

Daniel needed his friends' participation in seeking God's face, in order to know the king's dream and the interpretation of it. What if Daniel had despised the relationships before then? The end of the story may have been different. But Daniel had honored his covenant relationships, and together with his friends he accessed the Kingdom of God, and the dream and interpretation were revealed to them.

COVENANT RELATIONSHIPS ARE POWERFUL

I believe it is the dynamic of faith expressed through love that makes covenant relationships such a powerful key to winning behind enemy lines (see Gal. 5:6 NIV). There is such an atmosphere of love that exists among covenant partners, which causes their faith to attract the supernatural. For us to experience life on the level God wants us to, we must be walking by faith. We understand that faith pleases God (see Heb. 11:6). However, faith needs love in order to work. When two or more are gathered together in covenant relationship, there is an overflowing of the love of God in their midst. This love is the key to the activation of faith and the downloading of the presence of God.

When people who are in covenant with one another are together, there is usually a quickening of the spirit. I have experienced this myself very often. When I am with my covenant friends, it becomes easy for us to download the mind of God. The gifts of the Spirit are also manifested in a much greater dimension, and there is a release of grace from God's presence. When you are with such companions, things that could not happen if you were alone will happen.

A WORD OF CAUTION ABOUT
NON-COVENANT RELATIONSHIPS

Many people like to have friends or maintain friendships that have no spiritual connotations. They like hanging out with the "who's who," without regard for spiritual linkage. They are not even aware that they are victims of a master plan. Satan wants us in relationships that have no heart connection. Satan and his host war against every heart connection that the Spirit wants to establish between you and other

Christians. He also recognizes that when you can come into a heart connection with another believer, you have become a gateway for Heaven to show up on earth.

To weaken us, as individuals and the Church as a whole, the enemy tries to get us to play games. Hypocrisy and pretension are evidence or indications that this is occurring. We also should be concerned if everyone seems to be trying to impress one another, and there is no heart connection. If this is occurring, there will be a lack of spiritual substance and an absence of God.

Covenant companions will not be critical of you in a negative sense. They will have the freedom to correct and rebuke, but it will be done in love. Such companions will join with you to embrace the will of God for your life and together you will download the grace to move into God's purposes.

This is why we need to be wise about the company we keep. It is so easy to join the wrong company. All it takes is to allow external factors to motivate or influence us. So many "companies" are false. They look good on the outside but lack the substance of heart connections. If we allow what people possess financially or socially to motivate us in connecting with them, we are building on a shaky foundation.

COVENANT RELATIONSHIPS CREATE GODLY UNITY

Daniel went to his own company. God is calling aside His people, separating us from the world, and creating a covenant mind-set in us for exploits for His Kingdom. As I said before, when we are with our covenant companions (our own company), things that could not happen when we are alone will happen. The Bible says that when we are living together in unity, God bestows His blessings.

> *Behold, how good and how pleasant it is for brethren to dwell together in unity! It is like the precious oil upon the head, running down on the beard, the beard of Aaron, running down on the edge of his garments. It is like the dew of Hermon, descending upon the mountains of Zion; for there the Lord commanded the blessing—life forevermore* (Psalm 133 NKJV).

When we are in our own company, there is agreement, there is the unity of the Spirit, and brethren are dwelling together in unity! When we are with our covenant companions, we are confident. We know that we believe in each other, and we know we are looking out for the highest good for one another. We know such friends are forthright. Each of us has a relationship with God, but we are willing to come together because we know that in unity we are strengthened, edified, and brought closer to God.

When the Father, the Son, and the Holy Ghost are in the judgment seat in the creation room and they decide on something, it happens. When God sees the same kind of unity on earth, He is compelled to make His presence known. This is why satan fights covenant relationships. He fights unity. Satan creates a counterfeit of unity. He causes people to gather around political or doctrinal agendas in churches. This kind of unity cannot attract Heaven.

Covenant relationships must be created and fashioned by God. Man-made connections and unity cannot bring about the fulfillment of God's purposes. There must be a heart connection. The Holy Ghost will draw us from wherever we are, and He will join us to our own company. As He joins us to our own spiritual family, things that were formerly impossible will become possible.

Covenant relationships are a critical component for living victoriously. It is not enough to have a covenant relationship with God. We must also seek to have covenant relationships with others who can strengthen, encourage, and protect us. It is through such relationships that we will experience power and unity, and be able to grow and do more than we could have otherwise imagined.

"Furthermore, balance is possible when we are exposed to other people's insight and the Spirit of God bears witness with our spirits according to the truth of what they say. Paul's prayer in Ephesians 3 talks about being able to comprehend with all the saints what is the breadth, and length, and depth, and height of the love of Christ, which passes knowledge so that we might be filled with all the fullness of God (verses 18-19). This means that our full comprehension of God's love hinges on our receiving input from the insights others have from God. These dynamics are possible in covenant relationships.

I am almost certain that we have not explored sufficiently what God has made available to us through the right relationships He puts us in. Is it any wonder satan fights godly relationships?"

Relationships also require communication. While communication is necessary for any successful relationship, this is especially true regarding how we relate to God. We will look at this issue in the next chapter as we consider the importance of prayer.

CHAPTER SIX—HIGHLIGHTS AND WISDOM

- The Lord and Master, in His time of need, decided to call on those with whom He had a covenant relationship to help Him. By this, He set an example, showing that we need covenant relationships to walk victoriously in life.

- One of the weapons we can use to overcome is the covenant relationships that God has established around us. God put these relationships in place so that we may draw strength from these people even when we are weak.

- When people who are in covenant with one another are together, there is usually a quickening of the spirit.

- The Holy Ghost will draw us from wherever we are, and He will join us to our own company. As He joins us to our own spiritual family, things that were formerly impossible will become possible!

CHAPTER SEVEN

Prayer

Our ability to overcome the challenges of the day and beat the system of the world is dependent on a strong prayer life.

In warfare, communication and the ability to pass information accurately is vital. However, the importance of communication is not limited to wartime. The ability to pass and receive information is part of what keeps relationships going.

PRAYER ENABLES US TO BE AMBASSADORS FOR GOD

We always need to remember that though we live in the world, we are not of the world. We are citizens of the Kingdom of God, released into the world to overcome and to bring the kingdoms of the world under the lordship of Jesus

Christ. Just like Daniel, we are citizens of another land, operating as it were, in our own Babylon.

We have been placed in enemy territory to take over. God's plan is not for us to merely survive. God does not want His people hiding in caves! From the beginning, God's plan has been world dominion (see Gen. 1:26-28). Man is the agent God intends to use to bring His dominion on earth. For this to happen, our purpose and identity must be very clear to us. God created us in His image and likeness and released us on earth to express His will, person, and power as His representatives here on earth.

It is only when we have a clear understanding that we are representing the Kingdom of God on earth that the absolute importance of prayer becomes evident. Prayer is the means by which we stay in touch with our home base, understand the mind and will of the government we represent, and receive the grace and wisdom to execute the will of our government on earth.

We have been positioned behind enemy lines, and God has done this for a purpose. Our assignment is to exercise dominion on earth. By dominion, I mean making this earth what God intends it to be. In a sense, we are meant to colonize the earth. We are Heaven's representatives released on earth to make this world into what Heaven is like. This is one of the reasons why the Lord's Prayer states, "Your kingdom come. Your will be done on earth as it is in heaven" (Luke 11:2 NKJV). God wants His will done on earth, and we are on earth to see His will done.

We are like ambassadors representing the Kingdom of God on the earth. Just like any ambassador who knows what he or she is doing, we must maintain contact with our home government to know and understand the will and the policies of the government we represent. In addition, we must maintain open channels of communication so that resources can be sent to us when needed. This, among other things, is the role prayer plays in the life of a Christian.

We have examined Daniel's consecration, his knowledge of God, submission to authority, and understanding of covenant relationships. However, we must realize that the grace and knowledge Daniel had in these areas were born out of a life of intimacy with God, developed in the place of prayer.

Our ability to overcome the challenges of the day and beat the systems of the world is dependent on a strong prayer life. Can you imagine the kind of life an ambassador would have, if he did not stay in touch with the country he represents? Not only would he not know the will and the policies of his nation, he would also be cut off from the resources of the home country, which would normally be available to him.

PRAYER ENABLES US TO GAIN UNDERSTANDING

Daniel was a man of prayer. One of the prominent features of the story of Daniel, is the level of understanding Daniel was able to demonstrate as a result of a life of prayer. This quality is evident early in the Book of Daniel. In Daniel chapter 2, we read that King Nebuchadnezzar had a dream, which he refused to tell anyone and for which he demanded an interpretation. This was an impossible situation. No wisdom or understanding on earth could produce a solution. However, Daniel knew that all secrets belong to God. Daniel knew that the Kingdom he represented has no limits to the knowledge and understanding it can give its citizens. It is important to keep in mind that God gave the king the dream, and the Giver of dreams most certainly has the interpretation.

Yet although Daniel was a man in covenant with God, who had consecrated himself and refused the king's meat and wine, he did not know the king's dream or the interpretation. Also remember that at this time, Daniel already had friends (covenant relationships) and was walking in submission to authority. However, in spite of these things being in place in his life, Daniel did not automatically come to know the king's dream and the interpretation. He still had to employ a principle that we will examine in this chapter, and that is prayer.

> *He urged them to plead for mercy from the God of heaven concerning this mystery, so that he and his friends might not be executed with the rest of the wise men of Babylon. During the night the mystery was revealed to Daniel in a vision. Then Daniel praised the God of heaven...* (Daniel 2:18-19 NIV).

Daniel and his friends sought the face of God. They prayed, and it was in the place of prayer that the mystery was revealed to Daniel. This was just the beginning of many events and victories that Daniel experienced as a result of intimacy with God, which was developed in the place of prayer.

Prayer separates us from other people on earth. This is so because in prayer we demonstrate our allegiance and dependence on the Kingdom of God. I will say it again: We are a people in the world, but we are not of the world; our citizenship is of Heaven and Jesus is our King.

Prayer is not only a launching pad for our weapons of war; prayer itself is a powerful weapon that our King has given us to execute His will on earth. In prayer, we participate with our King to create the future He wants on earth, and to establish His Kingdom in the hearts of men. Prayer is man participating with God to see His will done on earth.

PRAYER ENABLES US TO RECEIVE KINGDOM RESOURCES

Prayer is the channel through which we maintain contact with our King and through which He releases Kingdom resources to us. In warfare, two of the primary targets are always the communication center and transport routes. Airports, bridges, boats, and supply convoys are identified as prime targets. The mind-set of any army is, "If we break communication and stop supplies, the enemy will be cut off and easy to destroy!" How true! An army that is cut off from its source—that has no supply channels—is an isolated army, easy to defeat. Natural armies recognize this and take extreme measures to guard communication centers and supply routes.

Prayer is the channel through which
we maintain contact with our King
and through which He releases
Kingdom resources to us.

Unfortunately, many in the Body of Christ have failed to understand the strategic importance of prayer. And unfortunately for them, the devil does! The Christian's prayer life is one of the first things the devil attacks, and he never stops attacking. The devil's mind-set is simple: Separate the Christian from the Kingdom he represents, and he can be easily destroyed.

THE EXAMPLE OF DANIEL IN PRAYER

Daniel's prayer life came under heavy attack in Daniel chapter 6. Here we see that the king chose Daniel to be one of his administrators. Daniel's job was to supervise the high officers and protect the king's interests, and he was quite successful. "Because of Daniel's great ability, the king made plans to place him over the entire empire" (Dan. 6:3 NLT). This did not sit well with the other administrators and high officers.

> Then the other administrators and high officers began searching for some fault in the way Daniel was handling government affairs, but they couldn't find anything to criticize or condemn. He was faithful, always responsible, and completely trustworthy. So they concluded, "Our only chance of finding grounds for accusing Daniel will be in connection with the rules of his religion." So the administrators and high officers went to the king and said, "Long live King Darius! We are all in agreement—we administrators, officials, high officers, advisors, and governors— that the king should make a law that will be strictly enforced. Give orders that for the next thirty days any person who prays to anyone, divine or human—except to you, Your Majesty— will be thrown into the den of lions. And now, Your Majesty, issue and sign this law so it cannot be changed, an official law of the Medes and Persians that cannot be revoked." So King Darius signed the law (Daniel 6:4-9 NLT).

Out of envy, prominent people in Babylon had tricked the king into making a decree. The decree was aimed at hitting the very essence of Daniel's success in the realm—his relationship with God. The Bible describes Daniel's success in detail:

> Daniel soon proved himself **more capable than all the other administrators** and high officers. **Because of Daniel's great ability, the king made plans to place him over the entire empire.** Then the other administrators and high officers began

*searching for some fault in the way Daniel was handling gov-ernment affairs, but they couldn't find anything to criticize or condemn. He was **faithful, always responsible,** and **completely trustworthy*** (Daniel 6:3-4 NLT).

Could it be that Daniel's enemies understood that Daniel's success stemmed from his relationship with God? Could it be they understood that the relationship was maintained and strengthened by regular communication and fellowship in the place of prayer? Could it be that they recognized that the wis-dom and excellence manifested in Daniel's life was released to him as he bowed his knees in prayer? Whatever they may have thought, they understood their enemy and launched an attack to hit Daniel at a point that could weaken and destroy him.

However, Daniel understood what the enemy was trying to do. Daniel also knew that his life and everything he had was a result of his relationship and contact with his King. So how did he respond?

But when Daniel learned that the law had been signed, he went home and knelt down as usual in his upstairs room, with its windows open toward Jerusalem. He prayed three times a day, just as he had always done, giving thanks to his God (Daniel 6:10 NLT).

The king's law had no effect on Daniel's actions. He con-tinued to pray, as was his custom. This lets us know that Daniel had always been a person of prayer, and he understood the importance of prayer.

WE NEED TO UNDERSTAND THE IMPORTANCE OF PRAYER

Most Christians are no longer aware of the importance of prayer. As a result, they are not even aware that they are under attack. Unlike in the days of Daniel, the world systems do not tell us not to pray. The world systems are designed in such a way to block us from praying.

A lot of people have been trapped by the world system (Babylon). They wake up early, rush to work, and come home tired late at night. Babylon has taken their time and squeezed them dry. No longer do they have quiet time or devotion. No longer is it possible to spend time with the King of kings. The demands of the world system make it impossible to pray.

Unlike Daniel, many Christians are not discerning enough to know this is an attack. They fail to recognize they are being systematically and strategically cut off from their source of life. Through the demands of the work place, many believers are being separated from the Kingdom they represent. Unknown to them, this is the way the enemy uses to strip them of their weapons and set them up for destruction.

We are behind enemy lines! We must wake up and realize that we are surrounded by the enemy. We are in a war zone. Our King has sent us behind enemy lines to launch an attack from within the enemy's territory and take over (see Mark 16:15). The only way we can defeat the enemy in his own territory is by maintaining contact with our Commander. Though we may be behind enemy lines, though we may be surrounded by the enemy, through prayer we establish a communication center and open a supply route between ourselves and our Kingdom.

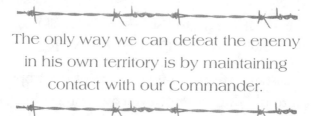

The only way we can defeat the enemy
in his own territory is by maintaining
contact with our Commander.

DEVELOPING A LIFESTYLE OF PRAYER

To win behind enemy lines, not only must we pray, we must develop a habit of prayer. It is not enough to pray when we are in trouble or when we have needs. We must have a disciplined pattern of regular prayer. Daniel had regular times of prayer (see Dan. 6:10).

Daniel did not rush into prayer because there was a situation in the kingdom. yet unfortunately, rushing into prayer is how we sometimes respond. I call it a "fire brigade" or "panic button" approach to prayer. In essence, when we face problems or difficulties, we sometimes treat prayer as a button to be pressed in panic. We pray only when we see a "five-alarm fire" in our lives.

We see prayer as a means to solving problems rather than an expression of a relationship. Consequently, when we don't see problems or when we think we can solve the challenges we face, we do not pray. This is not the mentality Daniel had. Neither should we embrace such a mind-set. For us to be successful and win in the world, we must develop a lifestyle of prayer.

Prayer has become a chore or religious obligation for some Christians, because the vital element of relationship has been removed. Unfortunately, some Christians lack what I call a vital relationship with God. A *vital relationship* is "an ongoing relationship that involves interaction and exchange between the parties involved." It is a real relationship whereby we are conscious of the presence, needs, and interests of the parties in the relationship.

Some Christians are lacking this vital relationship with the Father. Some think God is a distant old man who has rules and regulations that His children must strictly obey, or they will be punished immediately. For others God is God, but He is not really real to them! Yes, they believe He is out there, but He is not really involved. As a result, they cannot sense the consciousness of His presence and His willingness to interact. This is a mentality that makes prayer a religious duty, an obligation we just have to observe.

Recognizing that prayer is not a religious duty but an expression of a vital relationship transforms prayer into a joy and a delight. This makes prayer not just a duty but an opportunity to interact and fellowship with a loved one. It is only at this point that prayer can become a lifestyle, which it is meant to be.

PRAYER PROVIDES CLEANSING

Another reason why prayer must be a lifestyle is the very fact that we have been called to function behind enemy lines. As I've said many times, even though we are not of the world, we are in the world. Because we are in the world, every day of our lives we are being exposed to the influences of the world that we are called to live in and influence. This daily exposure allows deposits to be made on our souls, which need to be cleansed and washed away regularly.

In John chapter 13, Jesus took time out to wash the feet of His disciples (see John 13:1-17). It must be understood that in those days, the most common means of transportation was to walk. There were no motorcycles or cars. Although there were donkeys and horses, most people walked to get to the places they needed to go. In addition, the streets were not tarred or paved as they are today. The streets were very dusty and became muddy when it rained. The result of this state of affairs was that daily life necessitated regular washing of the feet. In going out and coming in, the dust and mud of the streets settled on the feet. Anyone who was active and going about his or her business would get dirty feet. At the end of the day or at intervals during the day, it was the responsibility of servants to wash the dirty feet of their masters.

Every day we wake up and go out. We go to work in a system that is contrary and alien to the things we believe and hold dear. As we go out daily into life, we are exposed to so many things that can contaminate or dirty our souls. The half-naked woman we see in the soap advertisement as we eat our lunch. The irritation and anger we feel toward our coworker in the office. The foul words and dirty jokes that we hear as we work in the factory or are at school. All these things leave a deposit on our soul that needs to be cleansed.

What Jesus did for His disciples is symbolic. Jesus, the living Word, washed the feet of His disciples. Likewise, we are cleansed with the washing of water by the Word. Ephesians chapter 5 describes how Christ loves the church and gave Himself up for it, "that He might sanctify and cleanse it with the washing of water by the word" (Eph. 5:26).

We must note that it was the disciples who were with Jesus who had their feet washed by Him. In essence, for a cleansing to take place, we must be in His presence. It was also the living Word that washed the feet of the disciples. What I am saying is that one of the ways we come into God's presence is through prayer. It is also in the place of prayer that the atmosphere is made conducive for the Holy Spirit to breathe upon the Word and make it come alive. Prayer creates the atmosphere needed for us to receive cleansing of our souls from the daily contamination to which we are exposed.

Because the exposure is daily, cleansing should be daily—meaning prayer should occur on a regular basis.

Defilement can give the enemy a place in us, but we must follow Jesus' example. Jesus said in John chapter 14, "Hereafter I will not talk much with you: for the prince of this world cometh, and hath nothing in Me" (John 14:30). This verse says that the prince of this world had nothing in Jesus; Jesus was not defiled or soiled in any way at all. This is one of the reasons He was totally effective in everything He did.

Jesus invaded an atmosphere laden with sin, a place under the influence of satan, and He was still victorious in all He did. Not for a moment do we see Jesus defeated. Jesus knew His Father's will! He spent much time in prayer. I also believe that by staying in the Father's presence, Jesus was able to stay free from the things that could have been a drag on His soul and a limitation to the call of God on His life. We must learn from the Master.

A life of prayer is not optional. We are behind enemy lines. We must stay pure and cleansed as we take over the territory God has given to us.

- We are citizens of the Kingdom of God, released into the world to overcome and to bring the kingdoms of the world under the lordship of Jesus Christ.

- Prayer is the means by which we stay in touch with our home base, understand the mind and will of the government we represent, and receive the grace and wisdom to execute the will of our government on earth.

- Prayer separates us from other people on earth. This is so because in prayer we demonstrate our allegiance and dependence on the Kingdom of God.

- Prayer is not only a launching pad for our weapons of war; prayer itself is a powerful weapon that our King has given us to execute His will on earth.

- Prayer is the channel through which we maintain contact with our King and though which He releases Kingdom resources to us.

- The world systems are designed in such a way to block us from praying.

- To win behind enemy lines, not only must we pray, we must develop a habit of prayer. It is not enough to pray when we are in trouble or when we have needs. We must have a disciplined pattern of regular prayer.

Conclusion

These endtimes demand a new kind of person, one who will be willing to pay the price so that God's will can come to pass in the earth. Daniel was God's man for his time. He *positioned* himself to be one of God's representatives in Babylon. His choices revealed his position under God for His glory. Daniel *purposed* in his heart not to defile himself with the delicacies of the king. He recognized the danger of defilement and was decisive about not being defiled. This is a quality that is necessary if we are going to succeed in these times. Daniel denied himself and risked losing everything good that he had going for him at the palace. He valued his God connection more than his comfort, convenience, or entertainment.

In Daniel, we see a man who humbled himself so God could exalt him in due course. In his relationships with those in authority over him, Daniel demonstrated real humility.

Daniel also enjoyed quality relationships with his companions. Covenant relationships are a major key to bringing about the expression of God's will on earth. Unity attracts God's blessing and power. (See Psalm 133 and Acts 2.) Covenant involves the laying down of lives. When people understand the power in covenant relationships, they will appreciate the power at their disposal for good to happen on earth.

A vital key in Daniel's life was undoubtedly his prayer life. Satan tried to weaken Daniel by keeping him from praying, but satan did not succeed. Prayer is the powerhouse for God's people on earth. It is often said that a prayerless Christian is a powerless one. We need to build a life of intimacy with God through our prayer life and our study life in Christ. The problem is not a lack of power from God but a lack of character developed in believers. Developing this character will enable us to receive the power that God is willing to release. Accurate praying can enhance character formation. Often failure in a Christian's life can be traced to a lack of prayer.

Wisdom was granted to Daniel, and he not only interpreted the king's dreams, but he was able to decode the plans of God in the last days. What an awesome privilege it is to know how to stand before God with no feeling of gross inadequacy—to know His plans, His purposes, and how to pursue them.

What we need to see in these days are not those who know how to argue, but those who know how to seek God; not just title lovers, but those who love to travail. We don't need glory seekers, but those who know how to groan. When the Daniels arise, they will travail and groan, seek the face of God, and see His will done on earth. They will be obedient like Jesus was to Father God, and they will give their all to see Him glorified. May you be like Daniel in these days!

The early Church in the Book of Acts demonstrated such strength and power in their time. We can see how they won behind enemy lines. Despite what seemed to be overwhelming odds, they were able to stand strong and advance the purposes of the Kingdom of God in their individual lives and in their corporate church experience. They faced opposition from the Jews (the religious leaders of their day), King Herod (the political/civil leaders), and even had to overcome economic hardship (see Heb. 10:34).

In Acts chapter 2, we see five key ingredients that cover all we have been studying in this book. These key ingredients as stated, summarize the message in this book. Some call it the five core experiences that make for strategic positioning for victory in these last days.

*And they continued stedfastly in the apostles' doctrine and fellowship, and in breaking of bread, and in prayers. And fear came upon every soul: and many wonders and signs were done by the apostles. And all that believed were together, and had all things common; and sold their possessions and goods, and parted them to all men, **as every man had need. And they, continuing daily with one accord in the temple, and breaking bread from house to house, did eat their meat with gladness and singleness of heart, praising God, and having favour with all the people. And the Lord added to the church daily such as should be saved** (Acts 2:42-47).*

The core experiences are as follows:

- Learning the Word.

- Worship through knowing and responding to God.

- Responsible involvement in serving others.

149

- Community (involvement with other like-minded people).

- Outreach (evangelism).

These experiences are interdependent, and each one influences and enriches the other.

LEARNING THE WORD

Early believers continued in the apostles' doctrine. They had a heart posture that enabled them to receive from the apostles. They demonstrated respect, submitted to their God-given authority, and were willing to learn and apply the truth of the Word of God. They were not just hearers of the Word but doers also.

The doing of the Word of God helps establish the Word in our lives and hearts. God uses His Word to enlighten us, give us direction in life, and strengthen us to do His will. The Word is a light unto our path and a lamp unto our feet. There are some internal attitudes that enhance or inhibit the effect of God's Word in the hearts of people. These believers had a right attitude and were eager to do the instructions derived from God's Word through their leaders: the apostles of Christ. Their consecration was a combination of their love for God, balanced with their reverence for Him.

WORSHIP THROUGH KNOWING AND RESPONDING TO GOD

Worship involves more than singing songs. It is our heart expression of how much God is worth to us, manifested in our daily lives through our thoughts, attitudes, and actions. It includes a value system that values God above all else. It is also a measure of our response to His goodness and mercy toward us. In John chapter 4, Jesus said the Father seeks worshippers who will worship Him in Spirit and truth (see John 4:23-24).

The first mention of the word *worship* in Scripture was when Abraham was going to offer Isaac, his son, in response to God's instruction. In Genesis 22, God instructs and Abraham obeys promptly, trusting in God to raise his son back according to Hebrews 11:17-19. The elements of worship are found in this account. It is initiated by God and involves: a heart of trust, placing more value on God than His gifts, a willingness to obey—whatever the cost—and a willingness to sacrifice what is so dear to us in response to God's demands on us. Even while going through such a test as this, Abraham still trusted in God's love and held onto His Word, knowing that what God promised, He would surely do. Abraham passed his tests and came into fulfillment of the promises of God.

Becoming a worshipper of God is to become a lover of God irrespective of any provision of material comfort. It attracts the presence of God. Worshippers will know God in a way that others may not. They will respond to Him in a different way and get results in a new dimension. When you have a group of worshippers, expect God's grace and power to be in ready manifestation.

RESPONSIBLE INVOLVEMENT IN SERVING OTHERS

This is the secret of covenant relationships: helping one another to be our best. In covenant relationships we are busy giving our best to build others up. The success of all is more glorious than the success of one. It is part of the effect of our individual relationship with God affecting our relationship one with another. Our individual gifting is discovered, developed, and deployed to bless others. The needs of others generate the desire to respond to those aspects of their corporate life.

The first commandment is to love God with all that is within us; the second is like the first—to love others, too (see Matt. 22:37-39). The first results in the second. The word *fellowship*, or *koinonia* in Greek, means among other things, "to participate, to share, to have in common, to have communion, to communicate, and to partake (take portions of) with one another of God's bountifulness."

COMMUNITY: LIKE-MINDED PEOPLE COMING TOGETHER

Whenever people come together to encourage the development, improvement, and well-being of one another, a community is formed. What they have can be called fellowship. In Scripture, fellowship is around God's Word and His Kingdom purposes. In the description found in Acts 2, the breaking of bread was the height of their fellowship, a time when they brought to their remembrance the finished work of Calvary—the shed blood and the broken body of Christ. They all shared what they had to meet the needs of each other. They were glad and had favor with outsiders. They had all things in common. They prayed for needs that were beyond their abilities to meet. God answered their prayers.

OUTREACH

The relational dynamic that existed among these early believers became a basis for attracting others into the fold. The Bible says God added to them "daily such as should be saved"

(Acts 2:47). They generated a godly influence in their time, and they not only survived but changed the course of events with their faith in God. Their influence brought great glory to God in their time, and many came to a saving knowledge of God in those places.

FINAL THOUGHTS

In the final analysis, this book has been about learning principles and developing skills in becoming key influencers for God in these times, rather than becoming victims of the decadence of our times. In both Old and New Testaments, we see how believers handled their challenges and prevailed behind enemy lines. The Bible says that the love of many will wax cold because iniquity shall abound (see Matt. 24:12).

We should not be those whose love will wax cold. We can have the testimony that when sin abounds, grace does much more abound. Defeat is not part of our inheritance; "we are not of them who draw back...but of them that believe to the saving of the soul" (Heb. 10:39). By His grace and mercy, coupled with our desire to love and obey, we shall be part of the glorious Church, without spot or wrinkle. Our prayer is that every reader will not just learn but be imparted with grace to win behind enemy lines.

Finally, I want to leave you with this thought. From the examples we see in the Bible, we know that those who overcome may be few in number. They may stand alone, at times. Consider Esther and Mordecai; consider Daniel and his friends; even Joseph stood alone. Even though they had to stand alone at times, their obedience usually brought great benefit and blessings not only for themselves but to others as well. All these people were instruments in the hands of God, who were used to bring about something greater that benefited God's people. Who knows, perhaps you are an Esther or Daniel.

I believe God is waiting for each of us to take our place so that His Kingdom can come on the earth. What are we waiting for? Let's hear His call and begin to dance to the music flowing from heavenly realms. God bless you as you heed His call.

Let us pray.

Father, we thank You for Your plans and purposes for our lives. We ask that every reader will come into the understanding of Your ways and be strengthened by Your grace to walk in obedience to You in all areas of our lives. May the spirit of truth breathe into us the wisdom and spiritual understanding needed for us to rise up and win over every situation we face in life. Help us, Lord, to be effective for You in bringing others to the knowledge of Your grace and truth so that many will be saved and come to the knowledge of the truth. Help us to be all You want us to be by Your word and by your Spirit. We pray this in the name of our Lord Jesus Christ. Amen.

Contact the Author

Mike Kola Ewuosho

Harvestime Church, Old Church Hall, Station Parade,
Virginia Water, Surrey GU25 4AB, UK
Phone number:+441344-844172

Word of Faith Christian Centre, 30 Nguru Road,
Nomansland, Kano, Box 13112 Kano, Nigeria

kola@fowm.org
http://www.fowm.org/
http://www.kolaewuosho.com/

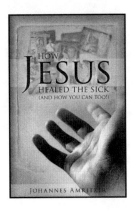